EXPLANATORY NOTES ON THE TREATISE:

Our Duty Concerning What Allāh Orders Us With

By Shaykh ul-Islām Muḥammad bin ʿAbdul-Wahhāb

Explanatory Notes By:
Shaykh ʿAbdur-Razzāq Ibn ʿAbdul-Muḥsin al- ʿAbbād al-Badr

ISBN: 978-1-6358-7511-9

First Edition: Rajab 1438 A.H. / April 2017 C.E.

Cover Design: Usul Designs

Translation by Abū Sulaymān Muḥammad 'Abdul-'Aẓīm Ibn Joshua Baker
Revision & Editing by 'Abdullāh Omrān

Typesetting & formatting by
Abū Sulaymān Muḥammad 'Abdul-'Aẓīm Ibn Joshua Baker

Printing: Ohio Printing

Subject: Minhāj/ 'Aqīdah

Website: www.maktabatulirshad.com
E-mail: info@maktabatulirshad.com

مكتبة الإرشاد
Maktabatul-Irshad
PUBLICATIONS

Table of Contents

BRIEF BIOGRAPHY OF THE AUTHOR

His name: Shaykh 'Abdur-Razzāq Ibn 'Abdul-Muḥsin al- 'Abbād al-Badr (حفظه الله)

He is the son of the *'Allāmah* and *Muhaddith* of Madīnah Shaykh 'Abdul-Muḥsin al 'Abbād al-Badr.

Birth: He was born on the 22nd day of *Dhul-Qa'dah* in the year 1382 AH in az-Zal'fi, Kingdom of Saudi Arabia. He currently resides in Madīnah.

Current Occupation: He is a member of the teaching staff at the Islāmic University of Madīnah.

Scholarly Certifications: Doctorate in *'Aqīdah*.

The Shaykh has authored books, papers of research, as well as numerous explanations in different disciplines. Among them are:

1. *Fiqh of Supplications & adh-Kār.*

2. *Hajj & Refinement of Souls.*

3. Explanation of 'Exemplary Principles' by Shaykh Ibn ʿUthaymīn (رَحِمَهُ ٱللَّهُ).

4. Explanation of the book, *The Principles of Names & Attributes*, authored by Shaykh-ul-Islām Ibn al-Qayyim (رَحِمَهُ ٱللَّهُ).

5. Explanation of the book, *Good Words*, authored by Shaykh-ul-Islām Ibn al-Qayyim (رَحِمَهُ ٱللَّهُ).

6. Explanation of the book, al-ʿAqīdah *at-Tahāwiyyah*.

7. Explanation of the book, *Fusūl: Biography of the Messenger*, by Ibn Kathīr (رَحِمَهُ ٱللَّهُ).

8. An explanation of the book, *al-Adab-ul-Mufrad*, authored by Imām Bukhārī (رَحِمَهُ ٱللَّهُ).

He studied knowledge under several scholars. The most distinguished of them are:

1. His father the *ʿAllāmah* Shaykh ʿAbdul-Muḥsin al-Badr (حفظه الله).

2. The ʿAllāmah Shaykh Ibn Bāz (رَحِمَهُ ٱللَّهُ).

3. The *ʿAllāmah* Shaykh Muḥammad Ibn Sālih al-ʿUthaymīn (رَحِمَهُ ٱللَّهُ).

4. Shaykh ʿAlī Ibn Nāsir al-Faqīhi (حفظه الله).

TRANSLITERATION TABLE

Consonants

ء	'	د	d	ض	ḍ	ك	k
ب	b	ذ	dh	ط	ṭ	ل	l
ت	t	ر	r	ظ	ẓ	م	m
ث	th	ز	z	ع	'	ن	n
ج	j	س	s	غ	gh	هـ	h
ح	ḥ	ش	sh	ف	f	و	w
خ	kh	ص	ṣ	ق	q	ي	y

Vowels

Short	َ	a	ِ	i	ُ	u
Long	ـَا	ā	ـِي	ī	ـُو	ū

Diphthongs	ـَو	aw	ـَي	ay

Arabic Symbols & their meanings

حفظه الله   May Allāh preserve him

رَضِيَاللَّهُعَنْهُ   May Allāh be pleased with him (i.e. a male companion of the Prophet Muḥammad)

سُبْحَانَهُوَتَعَالَى   Glorified & Exalted is Allāh

عَزَّوَجَلَّ   (Allāh) the Mighty & Sublime

تَبَارَكَوَتَعَالَى   (Allāh) the Blessed & Exalted

جَلَّوَعَلَا   (Allāh) the Sublime & Exalted

عَلَيْهِالصَّلَاةُوَالسَّلَامُ   May Allāh send Blessings & Safety upon him (i.e. a Prophet or Messenger)

صَلَّىاللَّهُعَلَيْهِوَعَلَىآلِهِوَسَلَّمَ   May Allāh send Blessings & Safety upon him and his family (i.e. Duʿā sent when mentioning the Prophet Muḥammad)

رَحِمَهُاللَّهُ   May Allāh have mercy on him

رَضِيَاللَّهُعَنْهُمْ

May Allāh be pleased with them (i.e. Du'ā made for the Companions of the Prophet Muḥammad)

جَلَّجَلَالُهُ

(Allāh) His Majesty is Exalted

رَضِيَاللَّهُعَنْهَا

May Allāh be pleased with her (i.e. a female companion of the Prophet Muḥammad)

ARABIC TEXT OF THE TREATISE

إِذَا أَمَرَ اللهُ الْعَبْدَ بِأَمْرٍ ، وَجَبَ عَلَيْهِ فِيهِ سَبْعُ مَرَاتِبَ : الْأُولَى : الْعِلْمُ بِهِ ، الثَّانِيَةُ : مَحَبَّتُهُ ، الثَّالِثَةُ : الْعَزْمُ عَلَى الْفِعْلِ ، الرَّابِعَةُ : الْعَمَلُ ، الْخَامِسَةُ : كَوْنُهُ يَقَعُ عَلَى الْمَشْرُوعِ خَالِصاً صَوَابًا ، السَّادِسَةُ : التَّحْذِيرُ مِنْ فِعْلِ مَا يُحْبِطُهُ ، السَّابِعَةُ : الثَّبَاتُ عَلَيْهِ

إِذَا عَرَفَ الْإِنْسَانُ : أَنَّ اللهَ أَمَرَ بِالتَّوْحِيدِ ، وَ نَهَى عَنِ الشِّرْكِ .

أَوْ عَرَفَ : أَنَّ اللهَ أَحَلَّ الْبَيْعَ وَ حَرَّمَ الرِّبَا . أَوْ عَرَفَ : أَنَّ اللهَ حَرَّمَ أَكْلَ مَالِ الْيَتِيمِ ، وَ أَحَلَّ لِوَلِيِّهِ أَنْ يَأْكُلَ بِالْمَعْرُوفِ إِنْ كَانَ فَقِيراً وَجَبَ عَلَيْهِ أَنْ يَعْلَمَ الْمَأْمُورَ بِهِ وَ يَسْأَلَ عَنْهُ إِلَى أَنْ يَعْرِفَهُ ، وَ يَعْلَمَ الْمَنْهِيَّ عَنْهُ ، وَ يَسْأَلَ عَنْهُ إِلَى أَنْ يَعْرِفَهُ .

وَاعْتَبِرْ ذَلِكَ بِالْمَسْأَلَةِ الْأُولَى ، وَ هِيَ : مَسْأَلَةُ التَّوْحِيدِ ، وَ الشِّرْكِ ؛ أَكْثَرُ النَّاسِ عَلِمَ أَنَّ التَّوْحِيدَ حَقٌّ ، وَ الشِّرْكَ بَاطِلٌ ، وَ لَكِنْ أَعْرَضَ عَنْهُ ، وَ لَمْ يَسْأَلْ . وَ عَرَفَ : أَنَّ اللهَ حَرَّمَ الرِّبَا ، وَ بَاعَ

وَاشْتَرَى وَ لَمْ يَسْأَلْ . وَ عَرَفَ : تَحْرِيمَ أَكْلِ مَالِ الْيَتِيمِ ، وَ جَوازَ الْأَكْلِ بِالْمَعْرُوفِ ؛ وَ يَتَوَلَّى مَالَ الْيَتِيمِ وَ لَمْ يَسْأَلْ .

الْمَرْتَبَةُ الثَّانِيَةُ : مُحَبَّةُ مَا أَنْزَلَ اللهُ ، وَ كُفِر مَنْ كَرَهَهُ ؛ لِقَوْلِهِ : ﴿ ذَلِكَ بِأَنَّهُمْ كَرِهُوا مَا أَنزَلَ ٱللَّهُ فَأَحْبَطَ أَعْمَٰلَهُمْ ۩ ﴾ [سُورَةُ مُحَمَّد] فَأَكْثَرُ النَّاسِ لَمْ يُحِبَّ الرَّسُولَ صَلَّى اللهُ عَلَيْهِ وَ سَلَّمَ ؛ بَلْ أَبْغَضَهُ ، وَ أَبْغَضَهُ ، وَ أَبْغَضَ مَا جَاءَ بِهِ ، وَ لَوْ عَرَفَ أَنَّ اللهَ أَنْزَلَهُ .

الْمَرْتَبَةُ الثَّالِثَةُ : الْعَزْمُ عَلَى الْفِعْلِ ؛ وَ كَثِيرٌ مِنَ النَّاسِ : عَرَفَ وَ أَحَبَّ ، وَ لَكِنْ لَمْ يَعْزِمْ ، خَوْفاً مِنْ تَغَيُّرِ دُنْيَاهُ .

الْمَرْتَبَةُ الرَّابِعَةُ : الْعَمَلُ ؛ وَ كَثِيرٌ مِنَ النَّاسِ إِذَا عَزَمَ أَوْ عَمَلَ ، وَ تَبَيَّنَ عَلَيْهِ مَنْ يُعَظِّمُهُ مِنْ شُيُوخٍ أَوْ غَيْرِهِمْ تَرَكَ الْعَمَلَ .

الْمَرْتَبَةُ الْخَامِسَةُ : أَنَّ كَثِيراً مِمَّنْ عَمَلَ ، لَا يَقَعُ خَالِصاً ، فَإِنْ وَقَعَ خَالِصاً ، لَمْ يَقَعْ صَوَاباً .

الْمَرْتَبَةُ السَّادِسَةُ : أَنَّ الصَّالِحِينَ يَخَافُونَ مِنْ حُبُوطِ الْعَمَلِ ؛

لِقَوْلِهِ تَعَالَى : ﴿ أَن تَحْبَطَ أَعْمَالُكُمْ وَأَنتُمْ لَا تَشْعُرُونَ

② ﴾ [سُورَةُ الْحُجُرَاتِ] ، وَ هَذَا مِنْ أَقَلِّ الْأَشْيَاءِ فِي زَمَانِنَا.

الْمَرْتَبَةُ السَّابِعَةُ : الثَّبَاتُ عَلَى الْـحَقِّ ، وَ الْـخَوْفُ مِنْ سُوءِ
الْـخَاتِمَةِ ؛ لِقَوْلِهِ صَلَّى اللهُ عَلَيْهِ وَ سَلَّمَ : ((إِنَّ مِنْكُمْ مَنْ
يَعْمَلُ بِعَمَلِ أَهْلِ الْـجَنَّةِ ، وَ يُـخْتَمُ لَهُ بِعَمَلِ أَهْلِ النَّارِ)) ، وَ
هَذِهِ أَيْضاً : مِنْ أَعْظَمِ مَا يَـخَافُ مِنْهُ الصَّالِحِينَ ؛ وَ هِيَ قَلِيلٌ
فِي زَمَانِنَا ؛ فَالتَّفَكُّرُ فِي حَالِ الَّذِي تَعْرِفُ مِنَ النَّاسِ فِي هَذَا وَ
غَيْرِهِ ، يَدُلُّكَ عَلَى شَيْءٍ كَثِيرٍ تَـجْهَلُهُ ؛ وَ اللهُ أَعْلَمُ .

INTRODUCTION

Indeed, all praises belong to Allāh. We praise Him, seek His aid, seek His forgiveness. We seek refuge with Allāh from the evil of our souls and the wicked consequences of our actions. Whomsoever Allāh guides, no one can mislead him and whomsoever is misled, no one can guide him.

I openly testify that no one has the right to be worshiped except Allāh alone Who has no partners. And I openly testify that Muḥammad is His servant and Messenger. May Allāh raise him in rank and grant his family and all his Companions peace.

To proceed:

The topic of this treatise is one of tremendous purpose which every Muslim, male and female, needs, **"Our duty concerning what Allāh orders us with."** Our duty concerning what we have been commanded with has been mentioned in the Book of our Lord (i.e., Allāh) and in the Sunnah of our Prophet (صَلَّى ٱللَّهُ عَلَيْهِ وَسَلَّمَ).

EXPLANATORY NOTES ON THE TREATISE: OUR DUTY
CONCERNING WHAT ALLĀH ORDERS US WITH

This lofty topic before us is a reminder that Allāh (عَزَّوَجَلَّ) did not make this creation futilely nor did he bring it into existence for play and amusement. Our Lord (i.e., Allāh) is free from that. Rather, He made the creation upon truth. Allāh (سُبْحَانَهُوَتَعَالَى) says,

$$ ﴾ خَلَقَ ٱلسَّمَٰوَٰتِ وَٱلْأَرْضَ بِٱلْحَقِّ تَعَٰلَىٰ عَمَّا يُشْرِكُونَ ٣ ﴿ $$

"He has created the heavens and the earth with truth. High be He Exalted above all they associate as partners with Him." [*Sūrah an-Nahl* 16:3]

Allāh (تَبَارَكَوَتَعَالَى) declared Himself above making this creation in falsehood or bringing it into existence for play throughout numerous verses in His Book. Allāh (سُبْحَانَهُوَتَعَالَى) says,

$$ ﴾ وَمَا خَلَقْنَا ٱلسَّمَاءَ وَٱلْأَرْضَ وَمَا بَيْنَهُمَا بَٰطِلًا ذَٰلِكَ ظَنُّ ٱلَّذِينَ كَفَرُوا۟ فَوَيْلٌ لِّلَّذِينَ كَفَرُوا۟ مِنَ ٱلنَّارِ ٢٧ أَمْ نَجْعَلُ ٱلَّذِينَ ءَامَنُوا۟ وَعَمِلُوا۟ ٱلصَّٰلِحَٰتِ كَٱلْمُفْسِدِينَ فِى ٱلْأَرْضِ أَمْ نَجْعَلُ ٱلْمُتَّقِينَ كَٱلْفُجَّارِ ٢٨ ﴿ $$

"And We created not the heaven and the earth and all that is between them without purpose! That is the consideration of those who disbelieve! Then woe to those who disbelieve (in Islāmic Monotheism) from the Fire! Shall We treat those who believe (in the Oneness of Allāh Islāmic Monotheism) and do righteous good deeds, as *Mufsidūn* (those who associate partners in worship with Allāh and commit crimes) on earth? Or shall We treat the *Muttaqūn* (pious - see V.2:2), as the *Fujjār* (criminals, disbelievers, wicked, etc.)?" [*Sūrah Sād* 38:27-28]

Allāh (سُبْحَانَهُوَتَعَالَى) clarifies this supposition and belief of the disbelievers in which they assume and believe they were only created for amusement, play, and in vain and that Allāh (سُبْحَانَهُوَتَعَالَى) only created this creation futilely. Meaning, without wisdom and purpose. Based upon this Allāh says,

"That is the consideration of those who disbelieve!"

Meaning those who assume this offense about the Lord of all that exists and believe this false creed about Him. Afterward, Allāh threatens them saying,

$$ \langle ۞ \; ﴾٢٧﴿ \; فَوَيْلٌ لِّلَّذِينَ كَفَرُوا۟ مِنَ ٱلنَّارِ ﴿ $$

"Then woe to those who disbelieve (in Islāmic Monotheism) from the Fire!"

Allāh (عَزَّوَجَلَّ) says in another verse,

$$ \langle وَمَا خَلَقْنَا ٱلسَّمَاءَ وَٱلْأَرْضَ وَمَا بَيْنَهُمَا لَٰعِبِينَ ﴿١٦﴾ لَوْ أَرَدْنَا أَن نَّتَّخِذَ لَهْوًا لَّٱتَّخَذْنَٰهُ مِن لَّدُنَّا إِن كُنَّا فَٰعِلِينَ ﴿١٧﴾ ﴾ $$

"We created not the heavens and the earth and all that is between them for a (mere) play. Had We intended to take a pastime (i.e. a wife or a son, etc.), We could surely have taken it from Us if We were going to do (that)." [*Sūrah al-Anbiyā* 21:16-17]

The Qur'ān mentions Allāh's (تَبَارَكَوَتَعَالَى) praise of His pious servants, His believing friends, and His close group who possess sound intelligence and an upright understanding. Among their momentous actions is their contemplation of the creation of the heavens and the earth as well as their firm 'Īmān, that it was not created futilely. Allāh says,

$$﴿ إِنَّ فِي خَلْقِ ٱلسَّمَٰوَٰتِ وَٱلْأَرْضِ وَٱخْتِلَٰفِ ٱلَّيْلِ وَٱلنَّهَارِ لَآيَٰتٍ لِّأُوْلِي ٱلْأَلْبَٰبِ ۝ ٱلَّذِينَ يَذْكُرُونَ ٱللَّهَ قِيَٰمًا وَقُعُودًا وَعَلَىٰ جُنُوبِهِمْ وَيَتَفَكَّرُونَ فِي خَلْقِ ٱلسَّمَٰوَٰتِ وَٱلْأَرْضِ رَبَّنَا مَا خَلَقْتَ هَٰذَا بَٰطِلًا سُبْحَٰنَكَ فَقِنَا عَذَابَ ٱلنَّارِ ۝ ﴾$$

"Verily! In the creation of the heavens and the earth, and in the alternation of night and day, there are indeed signs for men of understanding. Those who remember Allāh (always, and in prayers) standing, sitting, and lying down on their sides, and think deeply about the creation of the heavens and the earth, (saying): 'Our Lord! You have not created (all) this without purpose, glory to You! (Exalted be You above all that they associate with You as partners). Give us salvation from the torment of the Fire.'" [*Sūrah 'Āli 'Imrān* 3:190-191]

Meaning "This existence, and these people were not brought into existence futilely. You, O Allāh! Are exalted above and revered above that."

﴿ رَبَّنَا مَا خَلَقْتَ هَذَا بَاطِلًا سُبْحَانَكَ ﴾

"Our Lord! You have not created (all) this without purpose, glory to You!"

Meaning "Our Lord! We declare you above and glorified above what is falsely ascribed to You."

﴿ فَقِنَا عَذَابَ ٱلنَّارِ ۝ ﴾

"Give us salvation from the torment of the Fire."

So, they sought a means to request protection from the torment of the Fire from Allāh by declaring Him far above creating this creation futilely. This is a tremendous means of appealing to Allāh used by the people who believe in Allāh (تَبَارَكَوَتَعَالَى) to attain this request.

Within this, there is a great secret which must be noted:

This creed, the creed of the believers, **"that Allāh did not create this creation futilely"** has an effect on them in their actions, morals, demeanor, and worship. This creed raises them above nonsense, amusement, and futility which is in contrast to the purpose of being created. At the same time, the creed of the disbelievers **"that this creation was created with no purpose"** has an effect on them in their actions, morals, demeanor, and worship. This creed plunges them and drowns them in wasting time in amusement, to the point that their lives resembles that which is worse than the life of an animal.

On the other hand, the believer who believes that this creation was not brought into existence futilely and without purpose, his belief makes him strive seriously, work hard, and be energetic towards the reason why he was created and brought into existence and to actualize that purpose.

Whoever believes that the creation was created with no purpose and has this supposition will be thrown into the most severe destruction and ruin, in this life and the hereafter.

Based on this, the greatest means of appealing to Allāh (تَبَارَكَوَتَعَالَ), by requesting protection from the torment of the fire, has a deeply-rooted faith that Allāh did not create this creation without purpose. Rather, Allāh created it in truth and believing this truth results in the

believer doing righteous deeds, acts of obedience, and
having excellent nearness to Allāh (عَزَّوَجَلَّ).

The disbelievers who have this supposition about
Allāh are referred to within the statement of Allāh
(سُبْحَانَهُ وَتَعَالَ),

"That is the consideration of those who
disbelieve! Then woe to those who disbelieve
(in Islāmic Monotheism) from the Fire!" [*Sūrah
Sād* 38:27]

Allāh threatens them with the Fire on the Day of
Resurrection, that they will enter Hell and abide
therein for eternity. Based upon this, when they enter
the Fire on the Day of Resurrection and taste the
torment and all ways of escape will be cut off, Allāh
(سُبْحَانَهُ وَتَعَالَ) will say to them while they are there,

﴿ أَفَحَسِبْتُمْ أَنَّمَا خَلَقْنَكُمْ عَبَثًا وَأَنَّكُمْ إِلَيْنَا لَا تُرْجَعُونَ ۝ فَتَعَلَى ٱللَّهُ ٱلْمَلِكُ ٱلْحَقُّ لَاۤ إِلَهَ إِلَّا هُوَ رَبُّ ٱلْعَرْشِ ٱلْكَرِيمِ ۝ ﴾

"Did you think that We had created you in play (without any purpose) and that you would not be brought back to Us?" So, Exalted be Allāh, the True King, *La ilaha illa Huwa* **(none has the right to be worshiped but He), the Lord of the Supreme Throne!"** [*Sūrah al-Mu'minūn* 23:115-116]

Whoever analyzes the context mentioned in this verse at the ending of Sūrah al-Mu'minūn would understand that is a speech in which Allāh (تَبَارَكَ وَتَعَالَى) addresses the people of Hell on the Day of Resurrection while they are in Hell. This is because Allāh (سُبْحَانَهُ وَتَعَالَى) mentions the circumstance of people on the Day of Resurrection when they will be standing before the Lord of all that exists. They will come to Him (تَبَارَكَ وَتَعَالَى) divided into two groups, one group in Paradise and one in the Fire.

Allāh (تَبَارَكَ وَتَعَالَى) clarifies the circumstance of each group in these tremendous groups when He says,

﴿ فَإِذَا نُفِخَ فِي ٱلصُّورِ فَلَآ أَنسَابَ بَيْنَهُمْ يَوْمَئِذٍ وَلَا يَتَسَآءَلُونَ ۞ فَمَن ثَقُلَتْ مَوَٰزِينُهُۥ فَأُوْلَٰٓئِكَ هُمُ ٱلْمُفْلِحُونَ ۞ وَمَنْ خَفَّتْ مَوَٰزِينُهُۥ فَأُوْلَٰٓئِكَ ٱلَّذِينَ خَسِرُوٓاْ أَنفُسَهُمْ فِي جَهَنَّمَ خَٰلِدُونَ ۞ تَلْفَحُ وُجُوهَهُمُ ٱلنَّارُ وَهُمْ فِيهَا كَٰلِحُونَ ۞ أَلَمْ تَكُنْ ءَايَٰتِي تُتْلَىٰ عَلَيْكُمْ فَكُنتُم بِهَا تُكَذِّبُونَ ۞ قَالُواْ رَبَّنَا غَلَبَتْ عَلَيْنَا شِقْوَتُنَا وَكُنَّا قَوْمًا ضَآلِّينَ ۞ رَبَّنَآ أَخْرِجْنَا مِنْهَا فَإِنْ عُدْنَا فَإِنَّا ظَٰلِمُونَ ۞ قَالَ ٱخْسَـُٔواْ فِيهَا وَلَا تُكَلِّمُونِ ۞ إِنَّهُۥ كَانَ فَرِيقٌ مِّنْ عِبَادِي يَقُولُونَ رَبَّنَآ ءَامَنَّا فَٱغْفِرْ لَنَا وَٱرْحَمْنَا وَأَنتَ خَيْرُ ٱلرَّٰحِمِينَ ۞ فَٱتَّخَذْتُمُوهُمْ سِخْرِيًّا حَتَّىٰٓ أَنسَوْكُمْ ذِكْرِي وَكُنتُم مِّنْهُمْ تَضْحَكُونَ ۞ إِنِّي جَزَيْتُهُمُ ٱلْيَوْمَ بِمَا صَبَرُوٓاْ أَنَّهُمْ هُمُ

ٱلۡفَآئِرُونَ ۞ قَلَ كَمۡ لَبِثۡتُمۡ فِى ٱلۡأَرۡضِ عَدَدَ

سِنِينَ ۞ ﴾

"Then, when the Trumpet is blown, there will
be no kinship among them that Day, nor will
they ask of one another. Then, those whose
scales (of good deeds) are heavy, - these, they
are successful. And those whose scales (of good
deeds) are light; they are those who lose their
own selves, in Hell will they abide. The Fire
will burn their faces, and therein they will grin,
with displaced lips (disfigured). 'Were not My
Verses (this Qur'ān) recited to you, and then
you used to deny them?' They will say: 'Our
Lord! Our wretchedness overcame us, and we
were (an) erring people. Our Lord! Bring us out
of this; if ever we return (to evil), then indeed
we shall be Zālimūn: (polytheists, oppressors,
unjust, and wrong-doers, etc.).' He (Allāh) will
say: 'Remain you in it with ignominy! And
speak you not to Me! Verily! There was a party
of My slaves, who used to say: 'Our Lord! We
believe, so forgive us, and have mercy on us, for
You are the Best of all who show mercy!''
However, you took them for a laughingstock, so
much so that they made you forget My

Remembrance while you used to laugh at them!
Verily! I have rewarded them this Day for their
patience; they are indeed the ones that are
successful. He (Allāh) will say: 'What number
of years did you stay on earth?'" [Sūrah al-
Mu'minūn 23:101-112]

This speech is addressing the people of Hell, **"What
number of years did you stay on earth?"** How much
time did you spend in this world?

﴿ قَالُوا لَبِثْنَا يَوْمًا أَوْ بَعْضَ يَوْمٍ فَسْئَلِ ٱلْعَادِّينَ ۝ ﴾

**"They will say: 'We stayed a day or part of a day.
Ask of those who keep account.'"** [Sūrah al-
Mu'minūn 23:113]

Meaning ask the angels who kept account of our days,
deeds, and time.

﴿ قَٰلَ إِن لَّبِثْتُمْ إِلَّا قَلِيلًا لَّوْ أَنَّكُمْ كُنتُمْ
تَعْلَمُونَ ۝ أَفَحَسِبْتُمْ أَنَّمَا خَلَقْنَٰكُمْ عَبَثًا وَأَنَّكُمْ
إِلَيْنَا لَا تُرْجَعُونَ ۝ ﴾

**"He (Allāh) will say: 'You stayed not but a little,
if you had only known! Did you think that We**

had created you in play (without any purpose) and that you would not be brought back to Us?" [*Sūrah al-Mu'minūn* 23:114-115]

This is the speech in which Allāh (تَبَارَكَوَتَعَالَى) says to the people of Hell while they are there,

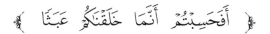

"Did you think that We had created you in play (without any purpose)?" [*Sūrah al-Mu'minūn* 23:115]

Meaning there is no wisdom or goal for being created. Is this how you should think about the Lord of all that exists - that Allāh brought this creation into existence for play without any purpose? This is the explanation of some of the scholars of Tafsīr concerning this verse.

Other scholars of Tafsīr say concerning the verse,

﴾ أَفَحَسِبْتُمْ أَنَّمَا خَلَقْنَاكُمْ عَبَثًا ﴿

"Did you think that We had created you in play (without any purpose)?" [*Sūrah al-Mu'minūn* 23:115]

Meaning "that you believed the only purpose I created you was for amusement and fun!"

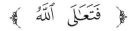

"So, Exalted be Allāh"

Meaning Exalted is Allāh above that.

"the True King"

The name *al-Haqq* (the Truth) is one of the Names of Allāh. Its meaning is the One Who there is no doubt concerning Him; not in His Essence, His Names, His Attributes, or in His Divinity. He is the One deserving to be worshiped without any partners.

Allāh (تَبَارَكَ وَتَعَالَى) is the Truth. His Names and Attributes are the truth. His actions and statements are the truth. His religion and legislation are true. All of His reports are true. His promise and the meeting with Him are true.

The Prophet (صَلَّى ٱللَّهُ عَلَيْهِ وَسَلَّمَ) use to commence his night prayer (*Tahajjud*) by acknowledging these meanings.

Just as that which is found in the Ḥadīth of Ibn ʿAbbas (رَضِيَاللّٰهُعَنْهُمَا), in which he said,

"That the Prophet (صَلَّىاللّٰهُعَلَيْهِوَسَلَّمَ) whenever he stood at night to pray *Tahajjud* (i.e., night prayer) he would say,

اللَّهُمَّ لَكَ الْحَمْدُ أَنْتَ قَيِّمُ السَّمَوَاتِ وَالْأَرْضِ وَمَنْ فِيهِنَّ، وَ لَكَ الْحَمْدُ أَنْتَ نُورُ السَّمَوَاتِ وَالْأَرْضِ وَمَنْ فِيهِنَّ ، وَلَكَ الْحَمْدُ أَنْتَ مَلِكُ السَّمَوَاتِ وَ الْأَرْضِ وَ مَنْ فِيهِنَّ ، وَ لَكَ الْحَمْدُ أَنْتَ الْحَقُّ وَوَعْدُكَ حَقٌّ، وَقَوْلُكَ حَقٌّ، وَلِقَاؤُكَ حَقٌّ، وَالْجَنَّةُ حَقٌّ، وَالنَّارُ حَقٌّ، وَالنَّبِيُّونَ حَقٌّ ، وَمُحَمَّدٌ صَلَّى اللهُ عَلَيْهِ وَ سَلَّمَ حَقٌّ ، وَالسَّاعَةُ حَقٌّ ، اللَّهُمَّ لَكَ أَسْلَمْتُ وَعَلَيْكَ تَوَكَّلْتُ وَبِكَ آمَنْتُ، وَإِلَيْكَ أَنَبْتُ، وَبِكَ خَاصَمْتُ، وَإِلَيْكَ حَاكَمْتُ، فَاغْفِرْ لِي مَا قَدَّمْتُ وَمَا أَخَّرْتُ، وَمَا أَسْرَرْتُ، وَمَا أَعْلَنْتُ، أَنْتَ الْمُقَدِّمُ وَأَنْتَ الْمُؤَخِّرُ لاَ إِلَهَ إِلاَّ أَنْتَ

Allāhumma laka al-ḥamdu anta qaiyyimus-samawati wal-ard wa man fihinna. Walakal-hamd, Laka mulkus-samawati wal-ard wa man fihinna. Walakal-hamd, anta nurus-samawati wal-ard. Wa lakal-hamd anta malikus-

*samawati wal-ard wa man fihinna. Wa lakal-
hamad anta-l-haqq wa wa'duka-lhaqq, wa
qawluka Haqq, wa liqa'uka Haqq, wal-jannatu
Han wan-naru Haqq wannabiyuna Haqq. Wa
Muḥammadun, sallal-lahu'alaihi wasallam,
Haqq, was-sa'atu Haqq. Allāhumma laka
aslamtu wabika amantu, wa 'Alayka
tawakkaltu, wa ilayka anabtu wa bika
khasamtu, wa ilayka hakamtu, faghfir li ma
qaddamtu wama akh-khartu wama as-rartu
wama'a lantu, anta-l-muqaddim wa anta-l-mu
akh-khir, la ilaha illa anta.*

'O Allāh! All the praises are for You. You are the
Sustainer of the heavens and the earth, and
whatever is in them. All the praises are for You.
You are the Light of the heavens, and the earth,
whatever is in them. All the praises are for You.
You are the Sovereign of the heavens and the
earth and whatever is in them. And all the
praises are for You. You are *al-Haqq* (the Truth),
and Your Promise is the Truth. Your Word is the
Truth And to meet You is true. Paradise is true,
And Hell is true. And all the Prophets are true,
And Muḥammad (ﷺ) is true. And the
Last Hour is true. O Allāh! I surrender (my will)
to You. I believe in You and depend on You and
repent to You. And with Your help, I argue with

my opponents, the disbelievers and I take You
as a judge (to judge between us). Please forgive
me my previous and future sins; and whatever I
concealed or revealed. And You are the One
Who makes (some people) forward and (some)
backward. None has the right to be worshiped
but You.'"[1]

The opposite of the truth is falsehood. It is used to
describe those objects of worship besides Allāh. Allāh
(جَلَّ وَعَلَا) says,

$$ \text{﴿ ذَٰلِكَ بِأَنَّ ٱللَّهَ هُوَ ٱلْحَقُّ وَأَنَّ مَا يَدْعُونَ} $$
$$ \text{مِن دُونِهِۦ هُوَ ٱلْبَٰطِلُ وَأَنَّ ٱللَّهَ هُوَ ٱلْعَلِيُّ} $$
$$ \text{ٱلْكَبِيرُ ۝ ﴾} $$

"That is because Allāh, He is the Truth (the only
True God of all that exists, Who has no partners
or rivals with Him), and what they (the
polytheists) invoke besides Him, it
is Bātil (falsehood) And verily, Allāh, He is the
Most High, the Most Great." [Sūrah al-Hajj 22:62]

---

[1] Collected by al-Bukhārī No. (1120, 6317, 7385, 7442, 7499); and
collected by Muslim No. (769). It is the first Ḥadīth mentioned in
the **book of at-Tahajjud** in Ṣaḥīḥ al-Bukhārī.

Likewise, an establishment of this great matter is mentioned in the Qur'ān. Allāh (جَلَّوَعَلَا) says,

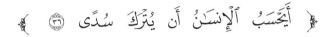

"Does man think that he will be left, *Suda* [neglected without being punished or rewarded for the obligatory duties enjoined by his Lord (Allāh) on him]?" [*Sūrah al-Qiyāmah* 75:36]

Does man believe that he was left, *Suda*? Some scholars say that the meaning of *Suda* is he will not be ordered or prohibited. Others say that it means that one will not be resurrected.

Ibn Kathīr (رَحِمَهُٱللَّهُ) said,

"What seems to be apparent about this verse is that it covers both circumstances. One will not be left in this worldly life without a purpose, without any commands or prohibitions. Nor will one be left in his grave without being resurrected. Rather, he will be ordered and prohibited in this worldly life and will be gathered and brought to Allāh in the Hereafter."[2]

---

[2] Tafsīr Ibn Kathīr (8/283).

Allāh (تَبَارَكَوَتَعَالَى) will resurrect mankind on the Day of Resurrection and they will stand before the Lord of all that exists, so that the good doers will be rewarded for their good and the bad doers will be punished for their evil. It is absurd that the Lord of all that exists will treat the good and evil person equally or the good and the wicked or the obedient and disobedient. Allāh (سُبْحَانَهُوَتَعَالَى) says,

$$\text{﴿ أَمْ نَجْعَلُ ٱلَّذِينَ ءَامَنُواْ وَعَمِلُواْ ٱلصَّٰلِحَٰتِ كَٱلْمُفْسِدِينَ فِى ٱلْأَرْضِ أَمْ نَجْعَلُ ٱلْمُتَّقِينَ كَٱلْفُجَّارِ ۝ ﴾}$$

"Shall We treat those who believe (in the Oneness of Allāh Islāmic Monotheism) and do righteous good deeds, as *Mufsidūn* (those who associate partners in worship with Allāh and commit crimes) on earth? Alternatively, shall We treat the *Muttaqūn* (pious - see V.2:2), as the *Fujjār* (criminals, disbelievers, wicked, etc.)?" [*Sūrah Sād* 38:28]

This will not happen. Rather, Allāh (تَبَارَكَوَتَعَالَى) is free from doing such things.

These verses, and those similar to it, illustrate the following:

❖ An awaking and enlightenment for the hearts.

❖ An alert for the heedless, a reminder for the believers, and an insight for the ignorant.

❖ A clarification of a great truth which one must keep in mind.

All of this, so one will not let years and days slip by, wasted in falsehood. For man was not created without purpose nor in vain.

Ibn Abū Hātim (رحمه الله) reported that a man from the family Sā'id Ibn al-'Ās (رحمه الله) said,

"The last sermon that 'Umar Ibn 'Abdul-Azīz gave, he praised and commended Allāh. Then he began by saying,

'To proceed: 'Indeed! You weren't created in vain. And surely you won't be left without commands or prohibitions. Verily, you have a Hereafter in which Allāh will descend to judge between you and divide you into groups. Those who do not have Allāh's mercy will be lost, ruined, and deprived of Paradise whose width is that of the heavens and earth. Don't you understand that no one will be safe in the Hereafter, except he who is cautious and fears that day, sells his worldly life for the hereafter, sells what is insignificant for what is abundant, sells fear (of the Dunya) for safety (in the Hereafter)? Don't you see that you are from the loins of those who have passed away. And those who come after you will remain until you return to the finest of inheritors (Allāh)? Afterward, everyday you will bid farewell, morning and night, to those who have passed away. Until you bury them in the earth. In the earth which is not smoothed nor cushioned. They will depart those whom they loved and plunge into the dirt. They will encounter their reckoning being subject to what they have done (of deeds), not in need of what they left behind (i.e. the worldly life), and in need of what they sent forth (of good deeds). So, fear Allāh, O servants of Allāh! Before one's covenant ends and death descends upon you.'

After he gave his sermon he placed the edges of his garment over his face and wept and those around him wept as well."

So, when the Muslim understands this matter and has certainty that he was not created without purpose and that Allāh (تَبَارَكَوَتَعَالَى) created him to be ordered and prohibited. What is the obligation concerning what Allāh orders and prohibits him with?

The subject of our decision here is:

The obligations which have been placed upon the Muslim, male and female, concerning what Allāh (تَبَارَكَوَتَعَالَ) orders us with are seven great matters. The Imām, the reviver, Shaykh ul-Islām Muḥammad Ibn 'Abdul-Wahhab (رَحِمَهُٱللَّهُ) clarified these seven matters in a concise treatise which has great and copious benefits.

What follows are the author's words which are in need of a brief explanation. The author (رَحِمَهُٱللَّهُ) said,

إِذَا أَمَرَ اللهُ الْعَبْدَ بِأَمْرٍ، وَجَبَ عَلَيْهِ فِيهِ سَبْعُ مَرَاتِبَ : الْأُولَى : الْعِلْمُ بِهِ ، الثَّانِيَةُ : مَحَبَّتُهُ : الثَّالِثَةُ : الْعَزْمُ عَلَى الْفِعْلِ ، الرَّابِعَةُ : الْعَمَلُ ، الْخَامِسَةُ : كَوْنُهُ يَقَعُ عَلَى الْمَشْرُوعِ خَالِصاً صَوَابًا ، السَّادِسَةُ : التَّحْذِيرُ مِنْ فِعْلِ مَا يُحْبِطُهُ ، السَّابِعَةُ : الثَّبَاتُ عَلَيْهِ

"When Allāh gives the servant a command, there are seven levels which one must take:

1. **Knowledge of it**

2. **Having love for it**

3. **Determination to act upon it**

4. Implementation

5. That it is sincerely for Allāh and upon the Sunnah

6. Cautioning against committing acts that will nullify deeds

7. Remaining firm upon it"

Explanatory notes

These matters are considered to be the essence of Islām which is a must to be meticulous in the following:

1. Preserving it
2. Comprehending it
3. Implementing it
4. Propagating it amongst the people.

Afterward, the author (رَحِمَهُٱللَّهُ) began by clarifying these matters in a concise manner with examples:

THE 1ST LEVEL KNOWLEDGE OF IT

Shaykh ul-Islām Muḥammad Ibn 'Abdul-Wahhāb
(رَحِمَهُٱللَّهُ) said,

إِذَا عَرَفَ الْإِنْسَانُ : أَنَّ اللَّهَ أَمَرَ بِالتَّوْحِيدِ ، وَ نَهَى عَنِ الشِّرْكِ .

أَوْ عَرَفَ : أَنَّ اللَّهَ أَحَلَّ الْبَيْعَ وَ حَرَّمَ الرِّبَا . أَوْ عَرَفَ : أَنَّ اللَّهَ

حَرَّمَ أَكْلَ مَالِ الْيَتِيمِ ، وَ أَحَلَّ لِوَلِيِّهِ أَنْ يَأْكُلَ بِالْمَعْرُوفِ إِنْ

كَانَ فَقِيراً وَجَبَ عَلَيْهِ أَنْ يَعْلَمَ الْمَأْمُورَ بِهِ وَ يَسْأَلَ عَنْهُ إِلَى أَنْ

يَعْرِفَهُ ، وَ يَعْلَمَ الْمَنْهِيَّ عَنْهُ ، وَ يَسْأَلَ عَنْهُ إِلَى أَنْ يَعْرِفَهُ .

وَاعْتَبَرَ ذَلِكَ بِالْمَسْأَلَةِ الْأُولَى ، وَ هِيَ : مَسْأَلَةُ التَّوْحِيدِ ، وَ الشِّرْكِ

؛ أَكْثَرُ النَّاسِ عَلِمَ أَنَّ التَّوْحِيدَ حَقٌّ ، وَ الشِّرْكَ بَاطِلٌ ، وَ لَكِنْ

أَعْرَضَ عَنْهُ ، وَ لَمْ يَسْأَلْ . وَ عَرَفَ : أَنَّ اللَّهَ حَرَّمَ الرِّبَا ، وَ بَاعَ

وَاشْتَرَى وَ لَمْ يَسْأَلْ . وَ عَرَفَ : تَحْرِيمَ أَكْلِ مَالِ الْيَتِيمِ ، وَ جَوَازَ

الْأَكْلِ بِالْمَعْرُوفِ ؛ وَ يَتَوَلَّى مَالَ الْيَتِيمِ وَ لَمْ يَسْأَلْ .

**"When one knows that Allāh orders Tawhīd
and forbids Shirk. Or he knows that Allāh has**

made lawful selling and made unlawful usury. Or that Allāh has made unlawful consuming the orphan's wealth and has made lawful that his guardian spends from the orphan's wealth accordingly if he is poor. So, it becomes mandatory for him to learn about what he is commanded with and ask about it in order to understand it. As well, it is mandatory upon him to learn about what he is forbidden to do and ask about it in order to understand it.

The first level can be illustrated in the example dealing with Tawhīd and Shirk. Many people know that Tawhīd is true and Shirk is false. However, they reject it and don't ask about it. They know that Allāh has made usury unlawful, yet they sell and buy (using it) and don't ask about it. They know the impermissibility of spending the orphan's wealth and the permissibility of spending accordingly, and they take possession of the orphan's wealth and don't ask concerning it."

Explanatory Notes on The Treatise: Our Duty Concerning What Allāh Orders Us With.

Explanatory notes

The first matter which is obligatory upon us
concerning what Allāh (تَبَارَكَوَتَعَالَى) orders us with is that
we learn about it (i.e. the order). This is the first
obligation, and it should start here. This is the reason
why Allāh (تَبَارَكَوَتَعَالَى) says,

$$ ﴾ فَٱعْلَمْ أَنَّهُ لَا إِلَهَ إِلَّا ٱللَّهُ وَٱسْتَغْفِرْ لِذَنۢبِكَ ﴿ $$

"So, know (O Muḥammad (صَلَّىٱللَّهُعَلَيْهِوَسَلَّمَ)) that *Lā
ilaha ill-Allāh* (none has the right to be
worshiped but Allāh), and ask forgiveness for
your sin." [*Sūrah Muḥammad* 47:19]

Hence, knowledge should be started before statements
and actions. If one doesn't seek knowledge of what
Allāh (تَبَارَكَوَتَعَالَى) orders or what He forbids, then how can
one do what he has been ordered with or turn away
from what is forbidden? As it has been said,

$$ فَاقِدُ الشَّيءِ لَا يُعْطِيهِ $$

"A person who doesn't have something cannot give it."

Or like it is said,

كَيْفَ يَتَّقِي مَنْ لَا يَدْرِي مَا يَتَّقِي ؟

"How can one protect himself from something if he doesn't know what it is that he is guarding himself against?" [3]

This is the reason why the first obligation concerning what Allāh (تَبَارَكَوَتَعَالَ) orders us with is to learn about it. And for the same reason, many verses and aḥādīth from our Messenger (صَلَّىٱللَّهُعَلَيْهِوَسَلَّمَ) encourage seeking knowledge, clarify its virtues, and mention its fruits and effects.

Among those statements is what our Prophet (عَلَيْهِٱلصَّلَاةُوَٱلسَّلَامُ) said,

مَنْ سَلَكَ طَرِيقًا يَلْتَمِسُ فِيهِ عِلْمًا سَهَّلَ اللَّهُ لَهُ طَرِيقًا إِلَى الْجَنَّةِ

---

[3] From the statement of Bakr bin Khunays which is reported by Abū Naʿīm in the book *al-Ḥilyah* (8/365).

"Whoever takes a path in search of knowledge, Allāh makes the path to Paradise easy for him." [4]

And the Prophet (ﷺ) said,

مَنْ يُرِدِ اَللَّهُ بِهِ خَيْرًا, يُفَقِّهْهُ فِي اَلدِّينِ

"When Allāh wishes good for anyone, He bestows upon him the Fiqh (comprehension) of the religion." [5]

It is authentically reported that our Prophet (عَلَيْهِ الصَّلَاةُ وَالسَّلَامُ) used to say every morning after the Fajr,

اللَّهُمَّ إِنِّي أَسْأَلُكَ عِلْمًا نَافِعًا وَرِزْقًا طَيِّبًا وَعَمَلاً مُتَقَبَّلاً

"O Allāh, I ask You for beneficial knowledge, goodly provision, and acceptable deeds." [6]

He would ask Allāh (تَبَارَكَ وَتَعَالَى) for that every day. Allāh says to him in the Qurʾān,

---

[4] Reported in Sahih Muslim No. (2699) from the Ḥadīth of Abū Hurayrah (رَضِيَ اللَّهُ عَنْهُ).
[5] Sahih al-Bukhārī No. (71); Sahih Muslim No. (1037) from the Ḥadīth of Muʿāwiyah bin Abū Sufyaan (رَضِيَ اللَّهُ عَنْهُ).
[6] Sunan ibn Majah No. (925) from the Ḥadīth of Umm Salamah (رَضِيَ اللَّهُ عَنْهَا). Shaykh Al-Albānī (رَحِمَهُ اللَّهُ) graded it Sahih.

$$ \langle\!\langle \quad \text{۱۱٤} \quad وَقُل رَّبِّ زِدْنِي عِلْمًا \quad \rangle\!\rangle $$

"And say: 'My Lord! Increase me in knowledge.'" [*Sūrah Tāhā* 20:114]

And the first verse revealed to Muḥammad (صَلَّىٱللَّهُعَلَيْهِوَسَلَّمَ) commanding him to read and learn was,

$$ \langle\!\langle \quad اقْرَأْ \quad \rangle\!\rangle $$

"Read!" [*Sūrah al-'Alaq* 96:1]

Carefully examine the previous supplication where the Prophet (صَلَّىٱللَّهُعَلَيْهِوَسَلَّمَ) began by asking for beneficial knowledge, before goodly provision or acceptable deeds. That is because beneficial knowledge aids the Muslim to distinguish between goodly provisions and unlawful provisions, between righteous and evil deeds. So how can one who doesn't have beneficial knowledge distinguish between the truth and falsehood and good and evil? Allāh (سُبْحَانَهُوَتَعَالَى) says,

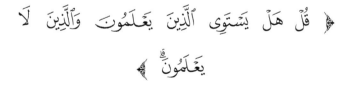

$$ \langle\!\langle \quad قُلْ هَلْ يَسْتَوِى ٱلَّذِينَ يَعْلَمُونَ وَٱلَّذِينَ لَا يَعْلَمُونَ \quad \rangle\!\rangle $$

"Say: 'Are those who know equal to those who
know not?'" [*Sūrah az-Zumar* 39:9]

And,

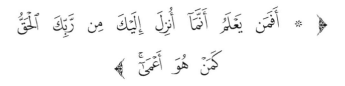

"Shall he then who knows that what has been
revealed unto you (O Muḥammad (صَلَّىٱللَّهُعَلَيْهِوَسَلَّمَ))
from your Lord is the truth be like him who is
blind?" [*Sūrah ar-Ra'd* 13:19]

Knowledge is a light for its companion. When he sets
out on his path with knowledge and insight of the
religion of Allāh (تَبَارَكَوَتَعَالَى), his footsteps will be correct.
In contrast to the one who works hard and strives
without knowledge and guidance.

'Umar Ibn 'Abdul-Azīz (رَحِمَهُٱللَّهُ) said about those
individuals,

"Whoever worships Allāh without knowledge
causes more corruption than rectification."[7]

---

[7] Reported by Ibn Abī Shaybah in the book *al-Musanif* No. (35098);
also, reported by ad-Dārimī in his *Sunan* No. (313); and Ibn Battah
reported it in the book *al-Ibānah* No. (579).

Innovation and various forms of falsehood didn't appear amongst the masses for any other reason except ignorance of Allāh's religion and worshiping without knowledge and insight!

Hence, knowledge is an enormous foundation and momentous pursuit which is incumbent upon every Muslim, male and female, to strive for. The scholars of Islām advise that the Muslim should seek a portion of knowledge throughout his entire day. Not a single day should pass him when he doesn't obtain some knowledge. Seeking knowledge is required of you daily. The evidence for that is clear in the supplication of our Prophet (صَلَّى ٱللَّهُ عَلَيْهِ وَسَلَّمَ) in which he said every morning after Fajr,

اللَّهُمَّ إِنِّي أَسْأَلُكَ عِلْمًا نَافِعًا

"O Allāh! I ask you for beneficial knowledge."

Based upon this, seeking knowledge should be present within the Muslim's daily schedule. He should set aside a portion of his day for acquiring knowledge.

Among Allāh's blessings is that in our era the means for obtaining knowledge have increased. You are able to listen to beneficial admonitions, lectures, speeches, Fatāwa, the Qur'ān, and Aḥādīth of the Messenger

EXPLANATORY NOTES ON THE TREATISE: OUR DUTY CONCERNING WHAT ALLĀH ORDERS US WITH

(صَلَّاللَّهُعَلَيْهِوَسَلَّمَ) in your car. Listening to blessed radio stations — the Noble Qur'ān radio station — which gathers knowledge and benefits many people throughout the world. Some esteemed individuals listen to a number of books with their explanations by the people of knowledge. The likes of this were not available in the early part of Islām.

What should be noted is that the first obligation upon us concerning what Allāh orders us with is to seek knowledge by learning about the commands and prohibitions.

Allāh orders us with Tawhīd, so we need to learn about it as it is the greatest of what Allāh orders us with. Likewise, Allāh orders us with the Salāh which is the greatest pillar of Islām after the two testimonies of faith. Thus, we need to learn about its conditions, pillars, obligatory matters. Didn't our Prophet (عَلَيْهِٱلصَّلَاةُوَٱلسَّلَامُ) say,

صَلُّوا كَمَا رَأَيْتُمُونِي أُصَلِّي

"Pray as you have seen me pray."[8]

---

[8] Sahih al-Bukhārī No. (631) on the authority of Mālik bin al-Hārith (رَضِيَٱللَّهُعَنْهُ).

How can the Muslim pray as the Messenger of Allāh (ﷺ) prayed without learning how he prayed?

Likewise, the same can be said about fasting, Zakāh, and all of the acts of obedience. The author (رَحِمَهُ ٱللَّهُ) then said,

وَاعْتَبَرَ ذَلِكَ بِالْمَسْأَلَةِ الْأُولَى ، وَهِيَ : مَسْأَلَةُ التَّوْحِيدِ ، وَ الشِّرْكِ ؛ أَكْثَرُ النَّاسِ عَلِمَ أَنَّ التَّوْحِيدَ ، وَ الشِّرْكَ بَاطِلٌ ، وَ لَكِنْ أَعْرَضَ عَنْهُ ، وَلَمْ يَسْأَلْ .

"The first matter can be illustrated in the example dealing with Tawhīd and Shirk. Many people know that Tawhīd is true and Shirk is false. However, they reject it and don't ask about it."

If you were to ask many people, "What do you think about Tawhīd?" they would say, "Tawhīd is good." And when they are asked, "What do you think about Shirk?" they would say, "Shirk is evil" however, one would not ask about Tawhīd or Shirk.

Based upon this, some Muslims do actions in total contradiction to Tawhīd. In reality, they are doing acts of Shirk. Yet they do not ask about Tawhīd, study it, get an understanding of it, or know about Shirk. As a result, one practices acts which are, in reality, acts of Shirk. This happens simply because it is an action which he doesn't ask about.

The author (رَحِمَهُ ٱللَّه) then said,

وَ عَرَفَ أَنَّ اللهَ حَرَّمَ الرِّبَا وَ بَاعَ وَاشْتَرَى وَ لَمْ يَسْأَلْ

"They know that Allāh has made usury unlawful, yet they sell and buy (using it) and don't ask about it."

Rather, some people, if they were to contemplate about asking about a lucrative deed, they would refrain from asking. They say, "Perhaps it is impermissible." So they won't ask about it, because they want to sell and buy. In this manner, they don't want to find out that it is impermissible because it would prevent him from this trade. It is common that people don't contemplate asking, even if it is said to them, "Ask." Rather, you find him reframing from asking.

The author (رَحِمَهُ ٱللَّه) then said,

وَ عَرَفَ : تَحْرِيمَ أَكْلِ مَالِ الْيَتِيمِ ، وَ جَوَازَ الْأَكْلِ بِالْمَعْرُوفِ ؛
وَ يَتَوَلَّى مَالَ الْيَتِيمِ وَ لَمْ يَسْأَلْ .

"They know the impermissibility of spending the orphan's wealth and the permissibility of spending accordingly, and they take possession of the orphan's wealth and don't ask concerning it."

One takes possession of the orphan's wealth without asking about the limits which authorize spending it. The Islāmic jurists state, "One is allowed to spend the lesser of two matters:

- A stipend similar to or
- According to one's needs.

However, the Islāmic jurists disagree whether it should be given back.

THE 2ND LEVEL: HAVING LOVE FOR IT

Shaykh ul-Islām Muḥammad Ibn ʿAbdul-Wahhāb (رَحِمَهُٱللَّهُ) said,

الْمَرْتَبَةُ الثَّانِيَةُ : مَحَبَّةُ مَا أَنْزَلَ اللهُ ، وَ كُفِرَ مَنْ كَرَهَهُ ؛ لِقَوْلِهِ : ﴿ ذَلِكَ بِأَنَّهُمْ كَرِهُواْ مَآ أَنزَلَ ٱللَّهُ فَأَحْبَطَ أَعْمَٰلَهُمْ ۝ ﴾ محمد: ٩ فَأَكْثَرُ النَّاسِ لَمْ يُحِبَّ الرَّسُولَ صَلَّى اللهُ عَلَيْهِ وَ سَلَّمَ ؛ بَلْ أَبْغَضَهُ ، وَ أَبْغَضَهُ ، وَ أَبْغَضَ مَا جَاءَ بِهِ ، وَ لَوْ عَرَفَ أَنَّ اللهَ أَنْزَلَهُ .

The second level is to have a love for what Allāh has revealed and whoever hates it has disbelieved. This is due to Allāh's statement,

"That is because they hate that which Allāh has sent down (this Qurʾān and Islāmic laws, etc.), so He has made their deeds fruitless." [*Sūrah Muḥammad 47:9*]

Many people do not really love the Messenger (ﷺ). Rather, they detest him and what he came with, even if they know that Allāh revealed it.

Explanatory notes

The second matter from what is obligatory upon us concerning what Allāh (تَبَارَكَ وَتَعَالَى) orders us with is that we fill our hearts with love for it. Having love drives us towards every good and calls us to every excellent quality. The Prophet (عَلَيْهِ الصَّلَاةُ وَالسَّلَامُ) said,

أَلاَ وَإِنَّ فِي الْجَسَدِ مُضْغَةً إِذَا صَلَحَتْ صَلَحَ الْجَسَدُ كُلُّهُ وَإِذَا فَسَدَتْ فَسَدَ الْجَسَدُ كُلُّهُ أَلاَ وَهِيَ الْقَلْبُ

"Beware! There is a piece of flesh in the body; if it is sound, the whole body is sound and if it is corrupt, the whole body is corrupt and that is the heart." [9]

---

[9] Sahih al-Bukhārī No. (52) and Sahih Muslim No. (1599) from the Ḥadīth of Nʿumān bin Bashīr (رَضِيَ اللَّهُ عَنْهُ).

Based upon this Ḥadīth, it is a must that the Muslim continuously fill his heart with having a love for Allāh, His Messenger (ﷺ), and His Legislation. One should work on fortifying this love in his heart and increasing its distance. For example, one loves the Ṣalāh, fasting, righteousness, keeping family ties, beneficence, and truthfulness. Likewise, one detests impermissible matters, sins, and abominations, etc.

When the heart loves for Allāh and hates for Allāh, one's circumstance becomes rectified. The Prophet (ﷺ) said,

مَنْ أَحَبَّ لِلَّهِ وَأَبْغَضَ لِلَّهِ وَأَعْطَى لِلَّهِ وَمَنَعَ لِلَّهِ فَقَدِ اسْتَكْمَلَ الْإِيمَانَ

"If anyone loves for Allāh's sake, hates for Allāh's sake, gives for Allāh's sake and withholds for Allāh's sake, he will have perfect faith."[10]

And,

---

[10] Sunan Abī Dāwud No. (4681) from the Ḥadīth of Abī Umāmah al-Bāhilī (رضي الله عنه). Shaykh al-Albānī (رحمه الله) graded it to be Ṣaḥīḥ in his book as-Saḥīḥah No. (380).

أَوْثَقُ عُرَى الْإِيمَانِ الْـحُبُّ فِي اللهِ، وَالْبُغْضُ فِي اللهِ

"The strongest handhold of faith is to love for Allāh and hate for Allāh."[11]

Based upon this, the Muslim continuously needs to strengthen in his heart the love for Allāh, His Messenger (صَلَّى ٱللَّهُ عَلَيْهِ وَسَلَّمَ), and His Legislation. One must exert all means which deepen one's love in the heart. One must also be diligent in removing the diseases from his heart.

Hence, because of one's heart deviating and becoming sick, you find some people not being devoted to good and being uneasy towards it. They are not happy to hear the good and they have tightness in their hearts when it is mentioned. On the other hand, when one with a sick heart is called to falsehood, he devotes himself to it and aspires for it. This is a perversion in the heart which Allāh (سُبْحَانَهُ وَتَعَالَى) says concerning it,

---

[11] Sharh as-Sunnah by Imām al-Baghawī No. (3468) from the Ḥadīth of Ibn 'Abbās (رَضِيَ ٱللَّهُ عَنْهُ). Shaykh al-Albānī (رَحِمَهُ ٱللَّهُ) graded it to be Saḥīḥ in his book as-Saḥīḥah No. (998).

﴿ رَبَّنَا لَا تُزِغْ قُلُوبَنَا بَعْدَ إِذْ هَدَيْتَنَا وَهَبْ لَنَا
مِن لَّدُنكَ رَحْمَةً إِنَّكَ أَنتَ ٱلْوَهَّابُ ۝ ﴾

**"(They say): 'Our Lord! Let not our hearts
deviate (from the truth) after You have guided
us, and grant us mercy from You. Truly, You are
the Bestower.'"** [*Sūrah ʿĀli ʿImrān* 3:8]

Based upon this, the servant is in need of having
diligence in filling his heart with love for Allāh, His
religion, His Legislation, and His commands. So, when
this love is present, one's circumstance is rectified.
Among the greatest recorded supplications from our
Prophet (ﷺ) is when he said,

أَسْأَلُكَ حُبَّكَ وَحُبَّ مَنْ يُحِبُّكَ وَحُبَّ عَمَلٍ يُقَرِّبُ إِلَى حُبِّكَ

**"I ask You for Your love, the love of whomever
You love, and the love of the deeds that bring
one nearer to Your love."[12]**

So, the Muslim should supplicate with this invocation,
reiterating it throughout one's life, and exerting all
means which fortify and increase the distance of his

---

12 Jāmiʿ at-Tirmidhi No. (3235) on the authority of Muʿādh bin
Jabal (ﷺ). At-Tirmidhi mentioned that this Ḥadīth is Hasan
Saḥīḥ.

love for Allāh, His Messenger, and His religion in his heart.

When acts of good become beloved to the heart, one devotes himself to them, seeks to act upon them, and carries them out. Islām requires from the servant to love deeds which bring one nearer to Allāh. Allāh (سُبْحَانَهُوَتَعَالَى) says in the Ḥadīth Qudsī,

وَمَا تَقَرَّبَ إِلَيَّ عَبْدِي بِشَيْءٍ أَحَبَّ إِلَيَّ مِمَّا افْتَرَضْتُهُ عَلَيْهِ، وَلَا يَزَالُ عَبْدِي يَتَقَرَّبُ إِلَيَّ بِالنَّوَافِلِ حَتَّى أُحِبَّهُ، فَإِذَا أَحْبَبْتُهُ كُنْت سَمْعَهُ الَّذِي يَسْمَعُ بِهِ، وَبَصَرَهُ الَّذِي يُبْصِرُ بِهِ، وَيَدَهُ الَّتِي يَبْطِشُ بِهَا، وَرِجْلَهُ الَّتِي يَمْشِي بِهَا، وَلَئِنْ سَأَلَنِي لَأُعْطِيَنَّهُ، وَلَئِنْ اسْتَعَاذَنِي لَأُعِيذَنَّهُ

"And My servant does not draw near to Me with anything more loved to Me than the religious duties I have obligated upon him. And My servant continues to draw near to me with nafil (supererogatory) deeds until I Love him. When I Love him, I am his hearing with which he hears, and his sight with which he sees, and his hand with which he strikes, and his foot with which he walks. Were he to ask [something] of Me, I would surely give it to him; and were he

to seek refuge with Me, I would surely grant
him refuge."[13]

On this occasion, one should take heed to the means
that bring about love which are ten:

1. Reading and contemplating over the Qurʾān
and its meanings. This should be done just as
one contemplates over a book that he is
memorizing and explains it in order to
comprehend what is intended by it.

2. Drawing nearer to Allāh by doing
supererogatory deeds after obligatory deeds.
This brings him to the level of those beloved by
Allāh after being on the level of having love.

3. Continuously remembering Allāh in all
circumstances with the tongue, the heart, and
actions. So, his portion of love is according to
his share in this remembrance.

---

13 Ṣaḥīḥ al-Bukhārī No. (6502) from the Ḥadīth Abī Hurayrah
(رَضِيَاللَّهُعَنْهُ).

4. Preferring loving Allāh over oneself when one's whims take over, and the raising of one's love for Allāh over one's whims is difficult.

5. The heart's study of Allāh's Names and Attributes. So, whoever studies about Allāh, His Names, Attributes, and Actions will inevitably love Him. Based upon this, the Mu'tazilah, Pharaonians, and Jahmiyyah are the highway robbers of the hearts that try to stop the hearts from obtaining the level of being beloved by Allāh.

6. Attesting to Allāh's kindness, beneficence, and apparent and not so apparent blessings invites to loving Allāh.

7. Among the most amazing is the state of being contrite before Allāh (سُبْحَانَهُۥوَتَعَالَى).

8. Being secluded in the last third of the night when Allāh descends to the lowest heaven in order to make secret supplication to Him, reciting His Speech, having *Fiqh* (understanding of the religion) within the heart, and refining one's worship before Allāh,

then concluding with seeking forgiveness and repentance.

9. Sitting with the beloved and truthful. Collecting the good features of their speech similarly to how the most excellent fruits are selected. You shouldn't speak except for what benefits, and understand that doing this increases your circumstance and benefits others.

10. Alienating from any means that prevent the heart from Allāh (جَلَّوَعَلَا).

So, these are the ten means that cause one to have a love for Allāh and attain the level of love that allows one to reach his Beloved. Its framework comprises to two matters:

1. Preparing the soul for this state.
2. Being open-minded to the essence of legislated knowledge and religious insight.

And to Allāh alone belongs success. [14]

---

[14] From the book *Madārij as-Saalikeen* by Ibn al-Qayyim (رَحِمَهُأللّٰه) (3/19).

The author (رَحِمَهُ ٱللَّهُ) then said,

وَ كُفر مَنْ كَرَهَهُ

"and whoever hates it has disbelieved."

Whoever detests anything that Allāh (سُبْحَانَهُوَتَعَالَى) revealed, this hatred renders his deeds fruitless. Allāh (سُبْحَانَهُوَتَعَالَى) says,

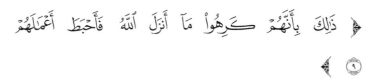

﴾ ذَلِكَ بِأَنَّهُمْ كَرِهُواْ مَآ أَنزَلَ ٱللَّهُ فَأَحْبَطَ أَعْمَلَهُمْ ﴿ ٩ ﴾

"That is because they hate that which Allāh has sent down (this Qurʾān and Islāmic laws, etc.), so He has made their deeds fruitless." [*Sūrah Muḥammad* 47:9]

Having hatred and anger for the religion of Allāh or for what Allāh (سُبْحَانَهُوَتَعَالَى) has legislated for His servants renders his deeds fruitless.

The author (رَحِمَهُ ٱللَّهُ) continues,

فَأَكْثُرُ النَّاسِ لَمْ يُحِبَّ الرَّسُولَ صَلَّى اللهُ عَلَيْهِ وَ سَلَّم

"Many people do not really love the Messenger (صَلَّى ٱللَّهُ عَلَيْهِ وَسَلَّم)."

True love emanates from the heart that adheres and treads on the methodology of the Messenger (ﷺ). Allāh (سُبْحَانَهُوَتَعَالَى) says,

$$﴿ قُلْ إِن كُنتُمْ تُحِبُّونَ ٱللَّهَ فَٱتَّبِعُونِي يُحْبِبْكُمُ ٱللَّهُ وَيَغْفِرْ لَكُمْ ذُنُوبَكُمْ ﴾$$

"Say (O Muḥammad (ﷺ) to mankind): 'If you (really) love Allāh then follow me (i.e. accept Islāmic Monotheism, follow the Qur'an and the *Sunnah*), Allāh will love you and forgive you of your sins.'" [*Sūrah 'Āli 'Imrān* 3:31]

One of the Salaf said,

$$لَيْسَ الشَّأْنُ أَنْ تُحِبَّ، وَلَكِنَّ الشَّأْنَ أَنْ تُحَبَّ$$

"The matter isn't that you love, rather it is that you are beloved."[15]

Meaning, that Allāh loves you. This cannot be obtained by mere claims. Based on this it was said,

$$تَعْصِي الْإِلَهَ وَأَنْتَ تَزْعَمُ حُبَّهُ$$

---

[15] Tafsīr Ibn Kathīr (2/32).

هَذَا لِعَمَرِي فِي الْقِيَاسِ شَنِيعٌ

لَوْ كَانَ حُبُّكَ صَادِقاً لَأَطَعْتَهُ

إِنَّ الْمُحِبَّ لِمَنْ أَحَبَّ مُطِيعُ

You disobey the One True Deity, yet you claim you love Him.

Within your analogy is a repugnant oath.

If your love was genuine you would have obeyed Him.

Verily, the one who truly loves is obedient to Whom he loves.

THE 3ᴿᴰ LEVEL: DETERMINATION TO ACT UPON IT

Shaykh ul-Islām Muḥammad Ibn 'Abdul-Wahhāb (رَحِمَهُ ٱللَّهُ) said,

الْمَرْتَبَةُ الثَّالِثَةُ : الْعَزْمُ عَلَى الْفِعْلِ ؛ وَ كَثِيرٌ مِنَ النَّاسِ : عَرَفَ وَ أَحَبَّ ، وَ لَكِنْ لَمْ يَعْزِمْ ، خَوْفاً مِنْ تَغَيُّرِ دُنْيَاهُ .

"The third level is to have the determination to act upon it (i.e. the order). Many people have studied and loved it; yet are not determined to act upon it out of fear of one's worldly life changing."

Explanatory notes

The third matter from what is obligatory upon us concerning what Allāh (تَبَارَكَوَتَعَالَى) orders us with is that we are determined to act upon it. Once you have

studied the command and have a love for it, you should now fix in your heart the determination to act upon it. Among the greatest supplications from our Prophet (صَلَّى اللهُ عَلَيْهِ وَسَلَّمَ),

اللَّهُمَّ إِنِّي أَسْأَلُكَ الثَّبَاتَ فِي الأَمْرِ وَالْعَزِيمَةِ عَلَى الرُّشْدِ

"O Allāh, I ask You for steadfastness in all my affairs and determination in following the right path...."[16]

To the end of the supplication.

Also, Ibn al-Qayyim (رَحِمَهُ اللَّهُ) commented on the previous Ḥadīth in his book *Miftāḥ Dār as-Saʿādah*,

وَ هَاتَانِ الْكَلِمَتَانِ هُمَا جِمَاعُ الْفَلَاحِ وَ مَا أُتِيَ الْعَبْدُ إِلَّا مِنْ تَضْيِيعِهِمَا أَوْ تَضْيِيعِ أَحَدِهِمَا

"These two words (i.e. steadfastness & determination) summarize true success and all of what the servant has been given save that he squanders both of them or one of them."[17]

---

[16] Reported by at-Ṭabarānī (رَحِمَهُ اللَّهُ) in the book *al-Mʿujam al-Kabeer* No. (7136) from the Ḥadīth of Shaddād ibn Aws (رَضِيَ اللَّهُ عَنْهُ). Shaykh al-Albānī (رَحِمَهُ اللَّهُ) graded it Saḥīḥ in his book *as-Saḥīḥah* No. (3228).
[17] (1/142)

Surely, the servant knows the right path and loves it. However, if his determination weakens, then his heart will not have devotion towards implementing action. For example, one learns about the Salāh and loves it. He knows its status and understands that it results in tremendous good and benefit in this life and the Hereafter. He also understands the punishment for the one who abandons it. Yet, when he has questioned himself about it and its status, he says, "I love it and don't detest it;" however, his determination has dwindled.

Likewise, he may listen to admonition and reminders, loves them and doesn't detest them; however, his determination is weak. Allāh (سُبْحَانَهُوَتَعَالَى) says,

$$ ﴿ وَلَوْ أَنَّهُمْ فَعَلُوا مَا يُوعَظُونَ بِهِۦ لَكَانَ خَيْرًا لَّهُمْ وَأَشَدَّ تَثْبِيتًا ۝ ﴾ $$

"But if they had done what they were told, it would have been better for them, and would have strengthened their (Faith)." [Sūrah an-Nisā' 4:66]

The author (رَحِمَهُٱللَّه) then said,

وَلَكِنْ لَمْ يَعْزِمْ ، خَوْفاً مِنْ تَغَيُّرِ دُنْيَاهُ .

**"Yet, are not determined to act upon it out of
fear of one's worldly life changing."**

For example, a person has a position of leadership,
wealth, or a great status and he fears it will change. Just
like the person who has status with the people of
innovation, then he learns about the Sunnah and loves
it. Yet, he hesitates from acting upon it and he does so
out of fear that his worldly life will change. Meaning
that he will lose this status and esteem. So, you find
him saying, "How can I act upon this matter! What will
those whom I have this great status with say about me!

THE 4ᵀᴴ LEVEL: IMPLEMENTATION

Shaykh ul-Islām Muḥammad Ibn 'Abdul-Wahhāb
(رَحِمَهُٱللَّهُ) said,

الْمَرْتَبَةُ الرَّابِعَةُ : الْعَمَلُ ؛ وَ كَثِيرٌ مِنَ النَّاسِ إِذَا عَزَمَ أَوْ عَمَلَ ،
وَ تَبَيَّنَ عَلَيْهِ مَنْ يُعَظِّمُهُ مِنْ شُيُوخٍ أَوْ غَيْرِهِمْ تَرَكَ الْعَمَلَ .

"**The fourth level is implementation (of the
order). Many people when they have the
determination or implement the action, those
who venerate him from the chiefs etc. would
discover it (from him) and he would abandon
the action.**"

Explanatory notes

The fourth matter is implementation. When you have
studied it, have a love for it, and are determined to act
upon it, you must do the action and persist in doing so.

Every deed has its proper time and you should beware of procrastinating and delaying. Rather, you should hasten and be swift in doing these deeds. Allāh (سُبْحَانَهُوَتَعَالَى) says,

$$ ﴿ ۞ وَسَارِعُوٓاْ إِلَىٰ مَغْفِرَةٍ مِّن رَّبِّكُمْ ﴾ $$

"And march forth in the way (which leads to) forgiveness from your Lord." [*Sūrah 'Āli 'Imrān* 3:133]

Also, in the Ḥadīth,

بَادِرُوا بِالأَعْمَالِ فِتَنًا كَقِطَعِ اللَّيْلِ الْمُظْلِمِ

"Be prompt in doing good deeds (before you are overtaken) by turbulence which would be like a part of the dark night."[18]

One should hasten and be swift. When the time of a deed approaches, he shouldn't delay. The Prophet (عَلَيْهِالصَّلَاةُوَالسَّلَامُ) was asked,

أَيُّ الْعَمَلِ أَحَبُّ إِلَى اللهِ ؟ قَالَ : الصَّلَاةُ إِلَى وَقْتِهَا

---

[18] Saḥīḥ Muslim No. (118) on the authority of Abū Hurayrah (رَضِيَاللَّهُعَنْهُ).

**"'Which of the deeds is loved most by Allāh?'
The Messenger of Allāh (صَلَّى اللَّهُ عَلَيْهِ وَسَلَّمَ) said, 'Salāh
at its proper time.'"[19]**

When the time of Salāh approaches, one should leave
off everything and hasten to it. Likewise, for every act
of obedience, one should be swift to perform it in its
proper time. He should accustom himself to being
persistent in implementation, having great concern for
acts of worship and obedience. One must be swift in
acting upon every deed in its proper time.

One should be on guard from distractions and
diversions. One must stay clear of any matter that will
divert him from doing deeds and keep him
preoccupied from acts of obedience which are the
purpose of his existence. Allāh (سُبْحَانَهُ وَتَعَالَى) says,

$$ ﴿ ۞ وَمَا خَلَقْتُ ٱلْجِنَّ وَٱلْإِنسَ إِلَّا لِيَعْبُدُونِ ﴾ $$

**"And I (Allāh) created not the jinns and humans
except they should worship Me (Alone)."** [*Sūrah
adh-Dhāriyāt* 51:56]

Then the author (رَحِمَهُ اللَّهُ) said,

---

[19] Saḥīḥ al-Bukhārī No. (527); and Saḥīḥ Muslim No. (85) on the
authority of Abdullāh bin Ma'sūd (رَضِيَ اللَّهُ عَنْهُ).

وَ تَبَيَّنَ عَلَيْهِ مَنْ يُعَظِّمُهُ

"Those who venerate him from the chiefs etc. would discover it (from him)."

Meaning, that they would become aware of him and it would become apparent to them concerning him. Some of the chiefs who hold him in high esteem would learn about his actions. The famous story of Heraclius, when he invited the heads of Rome and said to them,

يَا مَعْشَرَ الرُّومِ، هَلْ لَكُمْ فِي الْفَلَاحِ وَالرُّشْدِ وَأَنْ يَثْبُتَ مُلْكُكُمْ فَتُبَايِعُوا هَذَا النَّبِيَّ، فَحَاصُوا حَيْصَةَ حُمُرِ الْوَحْشِ إِلَى الْأَبْوَابِ، فَوَجَدُوهَا قَدْ غُلِّقَتْ، فَلَمَّا رَأَى هِرَقْلُ نَفْرَتَهُمْ، وَأَيِسَ مِنَ الْإِيمَانِ قَالَ رُدُّوهُمْ عَلَيَّ. وَقَالَ إِنِّي قُلْتُ مَقَالَتِي آنِفًا أَخْتَبِرُ بِهَا شِدَّتَكُمْ عَلَى دِينِكُمْ، فَقَدْ رَأَيْتُ. فَسَجَدُوا لَهُ وَرَضُوا عَنْهُ، فَكَانَ ذَلِكَ آخِرَ شَأْنِ هِرَقْلَ

"On that Heraclius invited all the heads of the Byzantines to assemble in his palace at Homs. When they assembled, he ordered that all the doors of his palace be closed. Then he came out and said, 'O Byzantines! If success is your desire and if you seek right guidance and want your

empire to remain, then give a pledge of allegiance to this Prophet (i.e. embrace Islām).'

On hearing the views of Heraclius, the people ran towards the gates of the palace like onagers, but found the doors closed. Heraclius realized their hatred towards Islām and when he lost the hope of their embracing Islām, he ordered that they should be brought back in audience.

When they returned, he said, 'What I already said was just to test the strength of your conviction and I have seen it.' The people prostrated before him and became pleased with him and this was the end of Heraclius's story (in connection with his faith)." [20]

So, when it became clear and manifested his affair, and they detested it, he feared his worldly life changing. Thus, he recanted his statement and remained upon his disbelief. The likes of this happens often.

---

[20] Ṣaḥīḥ al-Bukhārī No. (7) and (4553) on the authority of Ibn 'Abbās (رَضِيَاللَّهُعَنْهُ).

THE 5ᵀᴴ LEVEL: THAT IT IS SINCERELY FOR ALLĀH AND UPON THE SUNNAH

Shaykh ul-Islām Muḥammad Ibn 'Abdul-Wahhāb (رَحِمَهُأَللَّهُ) said,

الْمَرْتَبَةُ الْـخَامِسَةُ : أَنَّ كَثِيراً مِمَّنْ عَمَلَ ، لَا يَقَعُ خَالِصاً ، فَإِنْ وَقَعَ خَالِصاً ، لَمْ يَقَعْ صَوَاباً .

"The fifth level is that many people do deeds without sincerity to Allāh alone, and if it is done with sincerity to Allāh alone, it is not upon the Sunnah."

Explanatory notes

When the servant learns about the order, loves it, is determined to implement it, and acts upon it, he must aspire for sincerity in his deeds for Allāh alone. At the same time, his deeds must be in accordance with the

Sunnah of the Messenger of Allāh (صَلَّىٰاللَّهُعَلَيْهِوَسَلَّمَ). If the deed is not sincerely done for Allāh, it will not be accepted even if it is abundant. Allāh (سُبْحَانَهُوَتَعَالَىٰ) says in a Ḥadīth Qudsī,

أَنَا أَغْنَى الشُّرَكَاءِ عَنِ الشِّرْكِ؛ مَنْ عَمِلَ عَمَلًا أَشْرَكَ مَعِي غَيْرِي
، تَرَكْتُهُ وَشِرْكَهُ

"I am so self-sufficient that I am in no need of having an associate. Thus, he who does an action for someone else's sake, as well as Mine, will have that action renounced by Me to him whom he associated with Me."[21]

When the deed is not in accordance with the Sunnah, Allāh will not accept it. The Prophet (صَلَّىٰاللَّهُعَلَيْهِوَسَلَّمَ) said,

مَنْ عَمِلَ عَمَلًا لَيْسَ عَلَيْهِ أَمْرُنَا فَهُوَ رَدٌّ

"He who does an act which is not from our affair (i.e. Islām), it will be rejected (by Allāh)."[22]

So, deeds will not be accepted unless they are sincerely for Allāh and they are in accordance with the guidance

---

[21] Saḥīḥ Muslim No. (2985) from the Ḥadīth of Abū Hurayrah (رَضِىَاللَّهُعَنْهُ).
[22] Saḥīḥ al-Bukhārī No. (2697); and Saḥīḥ Muslim No. (1718) from the Ḥadīth of Āʾishah (رَضِىَاللَّهُعَنْهَا).

of the Noble Messenger (ﷺ). By these two conditions, deeds are good and accepted. Allāh (سُبْحَانَهُوَتَعَالَى) says,

"Who has created death and life, that He may test you which of you is best in deed. And He is the All-Mighty, the Oft-Forgiving." [*Sūrah al-Mulk* 67:2]

Al-Fuḍayl Ibn 'Iyāḍ (رَحِمَهُٱللَّهُ) said about the verse, "that He may test you which of you is best in deed,"

"'The most sincere and proper of them (i.e., deeds).' Someone asked him, 'O Abū 'Ālī! What does most sincere and proper of them (i.e. deeds) refer to?' Al-Fuḍayl said, 'Verily, deeds if they are sincerely for Allāh, yet not in accordance with the Sunnah, they are not accepted. And if they are in accordance with the Sunnah, yet not sincerely for Allāh, they will not be accepted either, until it is both."[23]

---

[23] In the book *Hilyah al-Awliyā* (8/95).

THE 6TH LEVEL: CAUTIONING AGAINST COMMITTING ACTS THAT WILL NULLIFY DEEDS

Shaykh ul-Islām Muḥammad Ibn 'Abdul-Wahhāb (رَحِمَهُٱللَّهُ) said,

الْمَرْتَبَةُ السَّادِسَةُ : أَنَّ الصَّالِـحِينَ يَخَافُونَ مِنْ حُبُوطِ الْعَمَلِ ؛

لِقَوْلِهِ تَعَالَى : ﴿ أَن تَحْبَطَ أَعْمَالُكُمْ وَأَنتُمْ لَا تَشْعُرُونَ

﴾ (٢) [سُورَةُ الْحُجُرَاتِ] ، وَ هَذَا مِنْ أَقَلِّ الْأَشْيَاءِ فِي زَمَانِنَا.

The sixth level is the righteous dread of their deeds becoming nullified and fruitless due to Allāh's Statement,

'Lest your deeds may be rendered fruitless while you perceive not.' [Sūrah al-Hujurāt 49:2]

And in our era, this is from the least of matters (i.e. that render deeds fruitless)."

Explanatory notes

Once you have studied it (i.e. an order), love it, are determined, act upon it, and perform the command with sincerity (to Allāh) and in accordance with the Sunnah of the Prophet (ﷺ), you must be on guard afterward from matters that could nullify and/or render your worship fruitless. Allāh (سُبْحَانَهُوَتَعَالَى) says,

"Lest your deeds may be rendered fruitless while you perceive not." [*Sūrah al-Hujurāt* 49:2]

Be on guard lest you perform a matter that will nullify your deed and render it fruitless. There are some people who will come on the Day of Resurrection with their deeds rejected and in vain.

The biggest nullifier and destroyer of deeds is associating partners with Allāh and disbelieving in Him. Allāh (سُبْحَانَهُوَتَعَالَى) says,

وَلَقَدْ أُوحِيَ إِلَيْكَ وَإِلَى ٱلَّذِينَ مِن قَبْلِكَ
لَئِنْ أَشْرَكْتَ لَيَحْبَطَنَّ عَمَلُكَ وَلَتَكُونَنَّ مِنَ
ٱلْخَاسِرِينَ ٦٥ بَلِ ٱللَّهَ فَٱعْبُدْ وَكُن مِّنَ
ٱلشَّاكِرِينَ ٦٦

"And indeed, it has been revealed to you (O
Muḥammad (صَلَّى ٱللَّهُ عَلَيْهِ وَسَلَّمَ)), as it was to those
(Allāh's Messengers) before you: 'If you join
others in worship with Allāh, (then) surely (all)
your deeds will be in vain, and you will
certainly be among the losers.' Nay! But
worship Allāh (Alone and none else), and be
among the grateful." [*Sūrah az-Zumar* 39:65-66]

And Allāh (جَلَّ وَعَلَا) says,

وَمَن يَكْفُرْ بِٱلْإِيمَانِ فَقَدْ حَبِطَ عَمَلُهُ وَهُوَ فِي
ٱلْآخِرَةِ مِنَ ٱلْخَاسِرِينَ ٥

"And whosoever disbelieves in the Oneness of
Allāh and in all the other Articles of Faith

[i.e. His (Allāh 's), Angels, His Holy Books, His Messengers, the Day of Resurrection and *Al-Qadar* (Divine Preordainments)], then fruitless is his work, and in the Hereafter, he will be among the losers." [*Sūrah al-Mā'idah* 5:5]

Thus, the servant must be on guard from actions that will nullify one's deeds. Showing off and seeking a reputation are actions that nullify one's deeds. For example, a person would do an action as a means of showing off or seeking a reputation among the people. In this example, one's intention isn't sincerely for Allāh (تَبَارَكَوَتَعَالَ) alone.

On this occasion, one must pay attention to the great amount of fear that the Companions (رَضِيَاللَّهُعَنْهُمْ) had for rendering their deeds nullified despite the perfection and state of their deeds.

Thābit bin Qays bin Shammās (رَضِيَاللَّهُعَنْهُ) was in a state of enormous fear because he thought he was included in the following verse,

﴿ لَا تَرْفَعُوا أَصْوَاتَكُمْ فَوْقَ صَوْتِ النَّبِيِّ وَلَا تَجْهَرُوا لَهُ بِالْقَوْلِ كَجَهْرِ بَعْضِكُمْ لِبَعْضٍ أَنْ تَحْبَطَ أَعْمَالُكُمْ وَأَنْتُمْ لَا تَشْعُرُونَ ۝ ﴾

"Raise not your voices above the voice of the Prophet (ﷺ), nor speak aloud to him in talk as you speak aloud to one another, lest your deeds may be rendered fruitless while you perceive not." [*Sūrah al-Hujurāt* 49:2]

And in the Ḥadīth,

عَنْ أَنَسِ بْنِ مَالِكٍ ـ رضى الله عنه ـ أَنَّ النَّبِيَّ صلى الله عليه وسلم افْتَقَدَ ثَابِتَ بْنَ قَيْسٍ فَقَالَ رَجُلٌ يَا رَسُولَ اللَّهِ أَنَا أَعْلَمُ لَكَ عِلْمَهُ. فَأَتَاهُ فَوَجَدَهُ جَالِسًا فِي بَيْتِهِ مُنَكِّسًا رَأْسَهُ فَقَالَ لَهُ مَا شَأْنُكَ. فَقَالَ شَرٌّ. كَانَ يَرْفَعُ صَوْتَهُ فَوْقَ صَوْتِ النَّبِيِّ صلى الله عليه وسلم فَقَدْ حَبِطَ عَمَلُهُ، وَهُوَ مِنْ أَهْلِ النَّارِ. فَأَتَى الرَّجُلُ النَّبِيَّ صلى الله عليه وسلم فَأَخْبَرَهُ أَنَّهُ قَالَ كَذَا وَكَذَا ـ فَقَالَ مُوسَى ـ فَرَجَعَ إِلَيْهِ الْمَرَّةَ الآخِرَةَ بِبِشَارَةٍ عَظِيمَةٍ فَقَالَ " اذْهَبْ إِلَيْهِ فَقُلْ لَهُ إِنَّكَ لَسْتَ مِنْ أَهْلِ النَّارِ، وَلَكِنَّكَ مِنْ أَهْلِ الْجَنَّةِ

THE 6TH LEVEL: CAUTIONING AGAINST COMMITTING ACTS THAT WILL NULLIFY DEEDS

"On the authority of Anas bin Mālik (رَضِيَ اللهُ عَنْهُ) that the Prophet (صَلَّى اللهُ عَلَيْهِ وَسَلَّمَ) missed Thābit bin Qays (رَضِيَ اللهُ عَنْهُ) for a period, so he inquired about him. A man said, 'O Allāh 's Messenger! I will bring you his news.' So, he went to Thābit and found him sitting in his house and bowing his head. The man said to Thābit (رَضِيَ اللهُ عَنْهُ), 'What is the matter with you?' Thābit (رَضِيَ اللهُ عَنْهُ) replied that it was an evil affair, for he used to raise his voice above the voice of the Prophet (صَلَّى اللهُ عَلَيْهِ وَسَلَّمَ) and so all his good deeds had been annulled, and he considered himself as one of the people of the Fire. Then the man returned to the Prophet (صَلَّى اللهُ عَلَيْهِ وَسَلَّمَ) and told him that Thābit (رَضِيَ اللهُ عَنْهُ) had said so-and-so. Musa bin Anas (رَضِيَ اللهُ عَنْهُ) said: 'The man returned to Thābit (رَضِيَ اللهُ عَنْهُ) with great, glad tidings. The Prophet (صَلَّى اللهُ عَلَيْهِ وَسَلَّمَ) said to the man. 'Go back to him and say to him: 'You are not from the people of the Hell-Fire, but from the people of Paradise.'"[24]

Another example is Thawbān (رَضِيَ اللهُ عَنْهُ) who narrated that the Prophet (صَلَّى اللهُ عَلَيْهِ وَسَلَّمَ) said,

[24] Saḥīḥ al-Bukhārī No. (4846) and (3613).

لَأَعْلَمَنَّ أَقْوَامًا مِنْ أُمَّتِي يَأْتُونَ يَوْمَ الْقِيَامَةِ بِحَسَنَاتٍ أَمْثَالِ

جِبَالِ تِهَامَةَ بِيضًا فَيَجْعَلُهَا اللَّهُ عَزَّ وَجَلَّ هَبَاءً مَنْثُورًا . قَالَ

ثَوْبَانُ : يَا رَسُولَ اللَّهِ صِفْهُمْ لَنَا جَلِّهِمْ لَنَا أَنْ لاَ نَكُونَ مِنْهُمْ

وَنَحْنُ لاَ نَعْلَمُ . قَالَ : أَمَا إِنَّهُمْ إِخْوَانُكُمْ وَمِنْ جِلْدَتِكُمْ

وَيَأْخُذُونَ مِنَ اللَّيْلِ كَمَا تَأْخُذُونَ وَلَكِنَّهُمْ أَقْوَامٌ إِذَا خَلَوْا

بِمَحَارِمِ اللَّهِ انْتَهَكُوهَا

"'I certainly know people of my nation who will
come on the Day of Resurrection with good
deeds like the mountains of Tihāmah, but Allāh
will make them like scattered dust.' Thawbān
(رَضِىَٱللَّهُعَنْهُ) said: 'O Messenger of Allāh, describe
them to us and tell us more, so that we will not
become of them unknowingly.' He (صَلَّىٱللَّهُعَلَيْهِوَسَلَّمَ)
said: 'They are your brothers and from your
race, worshipping at night as you do, but they
will be people who, when they are alone,
transgress the sacred limits of Allāh.'"[25]

The righteous are fearful of nullifying their deeds. The
difference between the righteous and unrighteous
pertaining to deeds is that the unrighteous perform

---

[25] Sunan ibn Majah No. (4245). Shaykh al-Albānī (رَحِمَهُٱللَّهُ) graded it
to be Saḥīḥ in his book as-Saḥīḥah (505).

deeds, then remind others of their good deeds as Allāh
(سُبْحَانَهُوَتَعَالَ) says,

"They regard as a favor upon you (O
Muḥammad (صَلَّىٰاللَّهُعَلَيْهِوَسَلَّمَ) that they have
embraced Islām. Say: 'Count not your Islām as
a favor upon me. Nay, but Allāh has conferred a
favor upon you, that He has guided you to the
Faith, if you indeed are true." [Sūrah al-Ḥujurāt
49:17]

Yet, when the righteous perform a deed they are
fearful that the deed will be nullified and not accepted
as Allāh (سُبْحَانَهُوَتَعَالَ) says,

$$\text{وَٱلَّذِينَ يُؤْتُونَ مَآ ءَاتَواْ وَّقُلُوبُهُمْ وَجِلَةٌ أَنَّهُمْ إِلَىٰ رَبِّهِمْ رَٰجِعُونَ ۝}$$

"And those who give that (their charity) which
they give (and also do other good deeds) with

their hearts full of fear (whether their alms and charities, etc., have been accepted or not), because they are sure to return to their Lord (for reckoning)." [*Sūrah al-Mu'minūn* 23:60]

Ā'ishah (رَضِيَاللَّهُعَنْهَا) said,

أَهُوَ الرَّجُلُ الَّذِي يَزْنِي وَيَسْرِقُ وَيَشْرَبُ الْخَمْرَ قَالَ " لاَ يَا بِنْتَ أَبِي بَكْرٍ - أَوْ يَا بِنْتَ الصِّدِّيقِ - وَلَكِنَّهُ الرَّجُلُ يَصُومُ وَيَتَصَدَّقُ وَيُصَلِّي وَهُوَ يَخَافُ أَنْ لاَ يُتَقَبَّلَ مِنْهُ

"Is this the one who commits adultery, steals and drinks alcohol?' He (صَلَّىَاللَّهُعَلَيْهِوَسَلَّمَ) said: 'No, O daughter of Abū Bakr – O daughter of Siddiq – rather, it is a man who fasts and gives charity and prays, but he fears that those will not be accepted from him."[26]

Allāh (سُبْحَانَهُوَتَعَالَى) says,

﴿ إِنَّمَا يَتَقَبَّلُ ٱللَّهُ مِنَ ٱلْمُتَّقِينَ ۝ ﴾

---

[26] Jāmi' at-Tirmidhi No. (3175); Sunan Ibn Majah No. (4198) with his wording. Shaykh al-Albānī (رَحِمَهُاللَّه) graded it to be Saḥīḥ in his book *as-Saḥīḥah* No. (162).

"Verily, Allāh accepts only from those who are *Al-Muttaqūn* (the pious - see V.2:2)." [*Sūrah al-Māʾidah* 5:27]

Meaning those who show piety to Allāh in the deeds which they establish. They perform it sincerely for Allāh alone and according to the Sunnah of the Prophet (ﷺ). Thus, the righteous fear nullifying their deeds.

The great second generation Muslim, Abdullāh bin Abī Mulaykah (رَحِمَهُ ٱللَّهُ) said,

أَدْرَكْتُ ثَلَاثِينَ مِنْ أَصْحَابِ النَّبِيِّ صَلَّى اللهُ عَلَيْهِ وَسَلَّمَ كُلُّهُمْ يَـخَافُ النَّفَاقَ عَلَى نَفْسِهِ .

"I met thirty Companions of the Prophet (ﷺ). All of them feared hypocrisy."

Al-Hasan al-Basrī (رَحِمَهُ ٱللَّهُ) said,

إِنَّ الْـمُؤْمِنَ جَمَعَ إِحْسَانًا وَ شَفَقَةً ، وَ إِنَّ الْـمُنَافِقَ جَمَعَ إِسَاءَةً وَ أَمْنًا

"Verily, the believer amasses perfection in deeds and fear; yet, the hypocrite amasses misdeeds and a false sense of security."[27]

The hypocrite performs deeds poorly while feeling safe that they will be accepted. As for the believer, he performs deeds with *Iḥsān* fearing that his deeds will be rejected.

The point here is that it is incumbent for the servant to be on guard from rendering his deeds fruitless.

---

[27] In the book *az-Zuhd* by Ibn al-Mubārak (رحمه الله) No. (985).

THE 7TH LEVEL: REMAINING FIRM UPON IT

Shaykh ul-Islām Muḥammad Ibn 'Abdul-Wahhāb (رَحِمَهُ ٱللَّهُ) said,

الْمَرْتَبَةُ السَّابِعَةُ : الثَّبَاتُ عَلَى الْـحَقِّ ، وَ الْـخَوْفُ مِنْ سُوءِ الْـخَاتِمَةِ ؛ لِقَوْلِهِ صَلَّى اللهُ عَلَيْهِ وَ سَلَّمَ : ((إِنَّ مِنْكُمْ مَنْ يَعْمَلُ بِعَمَلِ أَهْلِ الْـجَنَّةِ ، وَ يُـخْتَمُ لَهُ بِعَمَلِ أَهْلِ النَّارِ)) ، وَ هَذِهِ أَيْضاً : مِنْ أَعْظَمِ مَا يَـخَافُ مِنْهُ الصَّالِـحِينَ ؛ وَ هِيَ قَلِيلٌ فِي زَمَانِنَا ؛ فَالتَّفَكُّرُ فِي حَالِ الَّذِي تَعْرِفُ مِنَ النَّاسِ فِي هَذَا وَ غَيْرِهِ ، يَدُلُّكَ عَلَى شَيْءٍ كَثِيرٍ تَـجْهَلُهُ ؛ وَ اللهُ أَعْلَمُ .

The seventh step is to remain firm upon the truth, fearing a bad ending. This is due to the Prophet's (صَلَّىٰ ٱللَّهُ عَلَيْهِ وَسَلَّمَ) statement, 'Indeed, among you are those who do deeds from the people of Paradise; yet conclude with deeds from the people of Hell.' This is the greatest thing that

the righteous fear. Yet in our era, it is the least.
So, contemplating on the circumstance of those
you know concerning this matter and others
directs you toward a frequent matter which you
are unaware of, and Allāh knows best.

Explanatory notes

The seventh and last step from what is obligatory upon
us concerning what Allāh orders us with is to remain
firm. That one aspires to remain firm upon the truth,
guidance, and uprightness in the religion of Allāh until
his death.

Sufyān bin Abdullāh ath-Thaqafī (رَضِيَٱللَّهُعَنْهُ) said,

قُلْت: يَا رَسُولَ اللهِ! قُلْ لِي فِي الْإِسْلَامِ قَوْلًا لَا أَسْأَلُ عَنْهُ أَحَدًا
غَيْرَكَ؛ قَالَ: قُلْ: آمَنْت بِاَللَّهِ ثُمَّ اسْتَقِمْ

"I said, 'O Messenger of Allāh. Tell me
something about al-Islām which I can ask of

only you.' He (ﷺ) said, 'Say I believe in
Allāh — and then be steadfast.'"[28]

So, one should aspire for uprightness and remain firm
upon the religion of Allāh. One should continuously
ask Allāh (تَبَارَكَ وَتَعَالَى) that He keep him firm. Allāh
(سُبْحَانَهُ وَتَعَالَى) says,

$$﴾ يُثَبِّتُ ٱللَّهُ ٱلَّذِينَ ءَامَنُواْ بِٱلْقَوْلِ ٱلثَّابِتِ فِى$$
$$ٱلْحَيَوٰةِ ٱلدُّنْيَا وَفِى ٱلْأَخِرَةِ ﴿$$

"Allāh will keep firm those who believe, with
the word that stands firm in this world (i.e., they
will keep on worshipping Allāh Alone and
none else), and in the Hereafter." [*Sūrah 'Ibrāhīm*
14:27]

It is imperative for the Muslim to fear a bad ending.
The Prophet (ﷺ) said,

---

[28] Saḥīḥ al-Bukhārī No. (6594) and Saḥīḥ Muslim No. (6243) from
the Ḥadīth of Abdullāh bin Mas'ūd (رَضِيَ اللَّهُ عَنْهُ).

إِنَّ أَحَدَكُمْ لَيَعْمَلُ بِعَمَلِ أَهْلِ الْجَنَّةِ حَتَّى مَا يَكُونُ بَيْنَهُ
وَبَيْنَهَا إِلَّا ذِرَاعٌ فَيَسْبِقُ عَلَيْهِ الْكِتَابُ فَيَعْمَلُ بِعَمَلِ أَهْلِ النَّارِ
فَيَدْخُلُهَا

"Verily, one of you performs the actions of the people of Paradise until there is but an arm's length between him and it, and that which has been written overtakes him, and so he acts with the actions of the people of the Hell-Fire and thus enters it" [29]

Based on this, the Salaf would fear what is preordained and their last moments in this worldly life. The Prophet (ﷺ) said,

مَنْ كَانَ آخِرُ كَلاَمِهِ لاَ إِلَهَ إِلاَّ اللهُ دَخَلَ الْجَنَّةَ

"He whose last words are 'There is no deity worthy of worship except Allāh' will enter Paradise."[30]

---

[29] Ṣaḥīḥ al-Bukhārī No. (3208); and Ṣaḥīḥ Muslim No. (2643).
[30] Sunan Abi Dawud No. (3116) on the authority of Muʿādh bin Jabal (رضي الله عنه). Shaykh al-Albānī (رحمه الله) graded it to be Ṣaḥīḥ.

It is imperative for the Muslim to continuously beg Allāh (تَبَارَكَوَتَعَالَى) to keep him firm and not cause him to deviate.

Shahr bin Hawshab (رَضِيَاللَّهُعَنْهُ) said,

قُلْتُ يَا رَسُولَ اللَّهِ مَا لأَكْثَرِ دُعَائِكَ يَا مُقَلِّبَ الْقُلُوبِ ثَبِّتْ قَلْبِي عَلَى دِينِكَ قَالَ " يَا أُمَّ سَلَمَةَ إِنَّهُ لَيْسَ آدَمِيٌّ إِلاَّ وَقَلْبُهُ بَيْنَ أُصْبُعَيْنِ مِنْ أَصَابِعِ اللَّهِ فَمَنْ شَاءَ أَقَامَ وَمَنْ شَاءَ أَزَاغَ

"I said to Umm Salamah (رَضِيَاللَّهُعَنْهَا): 'O Mother of the Believers! What was the supplication that the Messenger of Allāh (صَلَّىاللَّهُعَلَيْهِوَسَلَّمَ) said most frequently when he was with you?' She (رَضِيَاللَّهُعَنْهَا) said: 'The supplication he said most frequently was: 'O Changer of the hearts, make my heart firm upon Your religion (Yā Muqallibal-qulūb, thabbit qalbī `alā dīnik).' She (رَضِيَاللَّهُعَنْهَا) said: 'So I said: 'O Messenger of Allāh, why do you supplicate so frequently: 'O Changer of the hearts, make my heart firm upon Your religion.' He (صَلَّىاللَّهُعَلَيْهِوَسَلَّمَ) said: 'O Umm Salamah! Verily, there is no human being except that his heart is between Two Fingers of the Fingers of Allāh, so

**whomever He wills He makes steadfast, and
whomever He wills He causes to deviate.'"[31]**

The Ḥadīth from Saḥīḥ al-Bukhārī and Muslim
mentions the supplication of our Prophet (ﷺ)
which he would say,

اللَّهُمَّ لَكَ أَسْلَمْتُ وَبِكَ آمَنْتُ وَعَلَيْكَ تَوَكَّلْتُ وَإِلَيْكَ أَنَبْتُ
وَبِكَ خَاصَمْتُ اللَّهُمَّ إِنِّي أَعُوذُ بِعِزَّتِكَ لاَ إِلَهَ إِلاَّ أَنْتَ أَنْ تُضِلَّنِي
أَنْتَ الْحَيُّ الَّذِي لاَ يَمُوتُ وَالْجِنُّ وَالإِنْسُ يَمُوتُونَ

**"O, Allāh! To You I have submitted, and in You
do I believe, and in You, I put my trust, to You
do I turn, and for You, I argued. O Allāh, I seek
refuge with You through Your Power; there is
none worthy of worship except You Alone; that
You safeguard me against going astray. You are
the Ever-Living, the One Who sustains and
protects all that exists; the One Who never dies,
whereas human beings and jinn will all die."[32]**

---

[31] Jāmi' at-Tirmidhī No. (3522) and he graded it to be Hasan.
Shaykh al-Albānī (رَحِمَهُ ٱللَّٰهُ) graded it to be Ṣaḥīḥ. Ṣaḥīḥ Muslim No.
(2654) from the hadith of Abdullāh bin 'Umar bin al-Aas (رَضِيَ ٱللَّٰهُ عَنْهُ).
[32] Ṣaḥīḥ al-Bukhārī No. (7383); Ṣaḥīḥ Muslim No. (2717) from the
Ḥadīth of Umm Salamah (رَضِيَ ٱللَّٰهُ عَنْهَا). Shaykh al-Albānī (رَحِمَهُ ٱللَّٰهُ) graded
it to be Ṣaḥīḥ.

Every time the Prophet (ﷺ) would leave his house, he would say,

اللَّهُمَّ إِنِّي أَعُوذُ بِكَ أَنْ أَضِلَّ أَوْ أُضَلَّ أَوْ أَزِلَّ أَوْ أُزَلَّ أَوْ أَظْلِمَ أَوْ أُظْلَمَ أَوْ أَجْهَلَ أَوْ يُجْهَلَ عَلَيَّ

"O, Allāh! I seek refuge in Thee lest I stray or be led astray, or slip or be made to slip, or cause injustice, or suffer injustice, or do wrong, or have wrong done to me."[33]

The point here is that the servant should invoke His Lord (Allāh) that he is not misled nor that he deviates. He should invoke His Lord that his heart is made firm on faith and that he takes the means to achieve firmness and uprightness in the religion.

From that is that one aspires continuously to rectify outwardly and inwardly the relationship between himself and Allāh. For this reason, the people of knowledge say, "It is unknown whether a person rectified himself inwardly and his 'Aqīdah is in order between himself and Allāh, even if his life is concluded with a bad ending."

---

[33] Sunan Abū Dawud No. (5094); Sunan Ibn Majah No. (3884) from the Ḥadīth of Umm Salamah (رَضِيَاللَّهُعَنْهَا). Shaykh al-Albānī (رَحِمَهُاللَّه) graded it to be Ṣaḥīḥ.

Abdul-Haqq al-Ishbīlī (رَحِمَهُ ٱللَّهُ) said,

> "Know that the bad ending—May Allāh give us
> refuge from it—doesn't occur to the one who is
> upright upon the religion outwardly and
> inwardly. This only happens to the one who has
> a corrupt intellect, persistently committing major
> sins, and embarking on crimes. Perhaps these
> things overtake him until death approaches him
> before he can repent. He is seized by death before
> he can rectify his intentions. Shaytān uproots him
> from this commotion (last moments of death),
> and seizes him at the time of his stupor."

What we need to take note of in the Ḥadīth is that the
person secretly has religious issues as the Prophet
(صَلَّى ٱللَّهُ عَلَيْهِ وَسَلَّمَ) said,

إِنَّ أَحَدَكُمْ لَيَعْمَلُ بِعَمَلِ أَهْلِ الْجَنَّةِ فِيمَا يَبْدُو لِلنَّاسِ

**"One of you performs deeds like the deeds of
the people of Paradise apparently before
people."[34]**

Based on this, it is a must that the servant is diligent in
rectifying his heart and purifying it with sincere

---

[34] Saḥīḥ al-Bukhārī No. (2898); Saḥīḥ Muslim No. (112) from the
Ḥadīth of Sahl bin Saʿd as-Sāʿidī (رَضِيَ ٱللَّهُ عَنْهُ).

devotion (to Allāh), truthfulness, love, and goodness. He should remove from his heart hate, rancor, hidden lusts, and resentment. Our Prophet (ﷺ) said in a supplication,

$$ وَاسْلُلْ سَخِيمَةَ قَلْبِي $$

"And O Allāh! Remove the treachery of my heart."[35]

The servant needs to rectify his heart and supplicate to His Lord (تَبَارَكَ وَتَعَالَى) that He makes him firm upon the truth and correct guidance. He needs to ask Allāh that He keeps him alive as a Muslim and causes him to die as a believer. He needs to ask Allāh to rectify his religion which is a protection for his affairs; and that Allāh rectifies his Hereafter which is his final abode. He needs to ask Allāh to make his life an increase for everything good and make his death an ease from everything evil.

In this same context, there are numerous invocations from our Prophet (ﷺ).

---

[35] Sunan Abū Dawud No. (1510); Jāmi' at-Tirmidhi No. (3551); Sunan Ibn Majah No. (3830) from the Ḥadīth of Ibn Abbas and Shaykh al-Albānī (رَحِمَهُ ٱللَّهُ) graded it to be Ṣaḥīḥ.

CLOSING

These seven matters are what is obligatory concerning what Allāh (تَبَارَكَوَتَعَالَ) orders us with.

I ask Allāh, the Lord of the Great Throne, to grant us success to actualize these seven matters; that He guide us to the Straight Path. May Allāh rectify all of our affairs and not leave us to handle it by ourselves for even the blink of an eye.

The last of our call is that all praise belongs to Allāh, the Lord of all that exists. May Allāh raise the rank of our Prophet and bestow blessings upon him, his family, and all his Companions.

Printed in Great Britain
by Amazon

83223788R00058